# THE LAW OF THE SEA
## IN A NUTSHELL

By

## LOUIS B. SOHN
Woodruff Professor of International Law
University of Georgia School of Law
Bemis Professor of International Law, Emeritus
Harvard Law School

and

## KRISTEN GUSTAFSON, J.D.

ST. PAUL, MINN.
WEST GROUP

Bancroft-Whitney • Banks-Baldwin • Clark Boardman Callaghan
Lawyers Cooperative Publishing • WESTLAW® • West Publishing

COPYRIGHT © 1984 By WEST PUBLISHING CO.

> 610 Opperman Drive
> P.O. Box 64526
> St. Paul, MN 55164–0526

**Library of Congress Cataloging in Publication Data**

Sohn, Louis B.
    The law of the sea in a nutshell.

    (Nutshell series)
    Includes index.
    1. Maritime law—United States.  2. Maritime law.
I. Gustafson, Kristen.  II. Title.  III. Series.
JX4422.U5S64   1984       341.4'5      84–7469

**ISBN** 0–314–82348–4

Sohn & Gustafson Law of Sea NS
4th Reprint–1998

# PREFACE

Two principles have governed the law of the sea since the early times when sailors and fishermen first ventured into the sea: the right of the coastal state to control a narrow strip along the coast, and the freedoms of navigation and fishing in the high seas beyond that coastal area. Some states made attempts to appropriate certain areas of the sea; Rome and later Venice claimed dominion over the Mediterranean, Great Britain over the North Sea, and Portugal and Spain over the seas adjoining America, Africa and southern Asia. The issue was settled in the "battle of the books" in the 1600's when the concept of the freedom of the sea, advocated by the Dutchman Hugo Grotius (de Groot), prevailed over the "closed seas" ideas of the Englishman John Selden. For 300 years there were only occasional challenges to the freedoms of the high seas, and the rules governing the exercise of these freedoms (especially the freedoms of navigation and fishing) were generally agreed upon. First the League of Nations in 1930 and then the United Nations in 1958 and 1960 tried to solve the one recurrent issue—the breadth of the territorial sea under the control of coastal states. Both efforts proved unsuccessful, but the United Nations was able to codify in four 1958 conventions many other rules governing the territorial sea and the high seas, and added new rules relating to the oil-rich continental shelf, the submerged part of the continents over which coastal states, led by the United States, started claiming jurisdiction in the 1940's.

The new treaties soon proved obsolete due to the rapid increase in the use of the ocean and in the exploitation of its resources. Fishing ceased to be a local enterprise, as large factory ships and vast fleets of smaller ships started roaming the oceans, exhausting the resources of one area after another. Mammoth oil tankers began carrying tremendous quantities of oil across the oceans, and several bad incidents made the people of the world conscious of the dangers of oil pollution of their beaches and fishing grounds. The marine environment could no longer cope with the assault from many directions: dumping of wastes from land, oil pollution from ships and additional oil pollution from drilling in the continental shelf. Technology developed to the point that even resources on the deep seabed, some 5,000 meters below the surface of the sea, became accessible, and a new regime became necessary for governing the exploitation of billions of tons of "manganese nodules," potato-sized lumps of several metals (not only manganese but also copper, nickel and cobalt), eagerly sought by metal-hungry industries.

Consequently in the late 1960's, the world was faced with a nightmare of conflicts over maritime rights between the big powers, between them and smaller powers, and between small powers themselves. The only possible solution was the establishment of a new international legal regime, a code of international law for the oceans. The United Nations arranged, therefore, for the Third United Nations Law of the Sea Conference, which over a period of eight years, 1974 to 1982, hammered out a convention on the subject, a complex document of almost 200 pages, some 400 articles (300 in the main text and 100 in annexes), containing provisions on fifteen major topics. The area covered is tremendous, more than 70 percent of the surface of the earth. In the final division of spoils, the coastal states were able to obtain jurisdiction (diminishing in proportion to distance from land) over the resources of one-third of the ocean area, and new rules, more precise than in the past, were developed to control navigation, fishing and exploitation of other resources of the sea, and to protect the marine environment from pollution.

The United Nations Convention on the Law of the Sea was finally signed in December 1982 at Montego Bay, Jamaica, by more than 120 countries, and a dozen of other countries signed it later. One country was conspicuously absent—the United States. The Reagan Administration, which in 1981 expressed some doubts about the compromises reached by previous United States Administrations with other countries, especially the developing countries, decided finally that the Convention was not acceptable to it, as some provisions relating to deep seabed mining were contrary to its philosophy and ideologically alien. Nevertheless, it announced that practically all the other provisions, especially those relating to international navigation and the rights and duties of coastal states, have by now become customary international law and as such binding on all states, whether parties to the Convention or not. In particular, in April 1983, President Reagan proclaimed a 200-mile wide exclusive economic zone, in terms consistent with the new Convention, and promised that the United States, subject to reciprocity, will respect similar zones established by other states. Consequently, it seems that, with the exception of the part relating to deep seabed mining, the provisions of the Convention have become the best evidence of the emerging new international law of the sea, and have become the law of the United States on the subjects covered by them. The Paquete Habana, 175 U.S. 677, 700 (1900) ("International law is part of our law, and must be ascertained and administered by the courts of the justice of appropriate jurisdiction, as often as questions of right depending upon it are duly presented for their determination. For this purpose, where there is no treaty and no controlling executive or legislative act or judicial decision, resort must be had to the customs and usages of civilized nations . . .").

In summarizing the current principles and rules of the law of the sea, this Nutshell relies, therefore, strongly on those parts of the United Nations Convention on the Law of the Sea which have been accepted by the United States. It takes into account also other relevant treaties of the United States (including the four 1958 conventions on the law of the sea ratified by the United States), United States legislation and the jurisprudence of the United States courts on this subject. It is hoped that this small volume would provide a sufficient introduction to this complex and vast subject for both students and for practicing lawyers. It must be remembered, however, that this volume can only highlight the principal issues, and anyone requiring more detailed knowledge on any particular topic would have to resort to the many monographs and law review articles on the subject.

## *Acknowledgements*

The authors are very grateful to Sharon Adams and Elizabeth Magee who typed and retyped the manuscript several times; to Judith Hatton who typed part of it and helped to edit the final draft; and to James W. King who proofread the book twice with an eagle eye and saved us from many mistakes.

LOUIS B. SOHN
KRISTEN GUSTAFSON

April, 1984

\*

# OUTLINE

## CHAPTER I. NATIONALITY OF VESSELS

## CHAPTER II. DUTIES AND JURISDICTION OF FLAG STATE AND RESTRICTIONS ON JURISDICTION OF STATES OVER FOREIGN VESSELS

## CHAPTER III.   THE BASELINE FOR DETERMINING ZONES OF NATIONAL JURISDICTION

## CHAPTER IV.   BOUNDARIES OF MARITIME JURISDICTION BETWEEN ADJACENT AND OPPOSITE STATES

## CHAPTER V. INTERNAL WATERS AND PORTS

## CHAPTER VI. THE TERRITORIAL SEA

# OUTLINE

## CHAPTER IX.   EXPLOITATION OF THE MINERAL RESOURCES OF THE DEEP SEABED

## CHAPTER X.   PROTECTION AND PRESERVATION OF THE MARINE ENVIRONMENT

XIV

# TABLE OF CASES

### References are to Pages

XV

# TABLE OF CASES

XVII

# TABLE OF CASES

# LOS CONVENTION TABLE

---

**References are to Pages**

---

# LOS CONVENTION TABLE

XXI

# LOS CONVENTION TABLE

# TABLE OF TREATIES

To avoid repetitive citations, this Table contains all of the relevant citations, arranged by treaty dates.

| Short Title | Full Title and Citation |
|---|---|
| 1783 United States—Great Britain Peace Treaty: | Definitive Treaty of Peace, United States—Great Britain, signed at Paris, Sept. 3, 1783, 8 Stat. 80, T.S. No. 104, 12 Bevans 8. |
| 1818 United States—Great Britain Fisheries Convention: | Convention Respecting Fisheries, Boundary, and Restoration of Slaves, United States—Great Britain, signed at London, Oct. 20, 1818, 8 Stat. 248, T.S. No. 112, 12 Bevans 57. |
| 1846 United States—Great Britain Boundary Treaty: | Treaty Establishing Boundary West of the Rockies (Oregon Treaty), United States—Great Britain, signed at Washington, June 15, 1846, 9 Stat. 869, T.S. No. 120, 12 Bevans 95. |
| 1882 North Sea Fisheries Convention: | Convention for Regulating the Police of the North Sea Fisheries, signed at The Hague, May 6, 1882, 160 Parry 219. |

XXIII

## TABLE OF TREATIES

# TABLE OF TREATIES

## TABLE OF TREATIES

XXVI

# TABLE OF TREATIES

# TABLE OF TREATIES

## TABLE OF TREATIES

# TABLE OF TREATIES

# TABLE OF TREATIES

# TABLE OF TREATIES

# TABLE OF TREATIES

# TABLE OF TREATIES

# TABLE OF TREATIES

# THE LAW OF THE SEA
## IN A NUTSHELL

*

# CHAPTER I

# NATIONALITY OF VESSELS

## A. INTRODUCTION

The concept of the freedom of the sea is based
on three basic principles: a ship of any state can
navigate the oceans freely; the state of the ship's
nationality has exclusive jurisdiction over the
ship on the high seas; no other state can exercise
jurisdiction over that ship. A ship's nationality
is, therefore, a crucial element of the regime of
the oceans.

"Nationality" is a term which has long been
used to define the legal relationship between a
state and a ship which is authorized by the state to
fly its flag. It is used in both the 1958 Convention
on the High Seas, Articles 5–6, and the Law of the
Sea (LOS) Convention, Articles 91–92. Several
national laws and international agreements refer
to the "registration" or "documentation" of a
ship rather than its nationality in describing the
special relationship between a ship and the state
under whose flag it sails (the "flag state"). Discussions in the International Law Commission in
1951 reflected concern that the use of the term
"nationality" in reference to ships was mislead-
ing as it implied similarity to the term's use in
defining the legal relationship between a state

and its citizen. U.N. Doc. A/CN.4/42 (1951); [1951] 1 Y.B. Int'l L. Comm'n 328–29. Nonetheless, the term has continued to be the one most often employed in describing the relationship between a ship and its flag state. It is important to realize, however, that in spite of their common names, the legal relationship ascribed to the nationality of ships does differ from that arising from the nationality of natural or juridical persons.

The concept of nationality of ships has developed over the centuries on lines parallel to those of the concept of freedom of the high seas:

> A corollary of the principle of the freedom of the seas is that a ship on the high seas is assimilated to the territory of the State the flag of which it flies, for, just as in its own territory, that State exercises its authority upon it, and no other State may do so.

The S.S. Lotus, P.C.I.J., Ser. A, No. 10, at 25 (1927).

Absence of nationality practically precludes a ship from engaging in international trade or commerce or navigation of any sort on the high seas. Any state can board and assert its jurisdiction over a stateless ship on the high seas. LOS Convention, Article 110(1)(d). See also Anderson, "Jurisdiction over Stateless Vessels on the High Seas," 13 J.Mar.L. & Com. 323 (1982). Furthermore, the ship would not be able to benefit from treaties on which rights to enter foreign ports are normally based. See, for example, 1956 United States-Netherlands Treaty of Friendship, Commerce and Navigation, Article 19(2).

Each nation has the right to confer its nationality on a ship, though only after World War II was it recognized that a landlocked state may also have ships sailing under its flag. 1919 Treaty of Peace with Germany, Article 273; 1958 Convention on the High Seas, Article 4; LOS Convention, Article 90. International organizations, such as the United Nations and its agencies, may sail vessels under their flag. 1958 Convention on the High Seas, Article 7; LOS Convention, Article 93. Ordinarily a state confers its nationality on a ship by registering the ship, authorizing it to fly its flag, and issuing documents evidencing the ship's nationality. A ship may fly the flag of one state only. 1958 Convention on the High Seas, Article 6(1); LOS Convention, Article 92(1).

## B. THE RIGHT OF STATES TO CONFER NATIONALITY UPON A SHIP

### 1. *General Principle*

In the Muscat Dhows Case, the Permanent Court of Arbitration pronounced the generally accepted principle that "it belongs to every sover-

eign to decide to whom he will accord the right
to fly his flag and to prescribe the rules governing such grants." Scott, The Hague Court Reports 93, 96 (1916). The U.S. Supreme Court re-
iterated this principle, stating that "[e]ach state
under international law may determine for itself
the conditions on which it will grant its nationality to a merchant ship." Lauritzen v. Larsen, 345
U.S. 571, 584 (1953). Numerous treaties and international agreements have incorporated this
principle; for instance, the 1956 United States-
Netherlands Treaty of Friendship, Commerce and
Navigation, provides in Article 19(1) that "[v]es-
sels under the flag of either Party, and carrying
the papers required by its laws in proof of nationality, shall be deemed to be vessels of that Party
both on the high seas and within the ports, places
and waters of the other Party."

## 2. *Limitations*

International law has developed certain limitations on a state's unilateral right to confer its
nationality upon a ship. One such limitation is
the principle prohibiting a state from granting
its nationality to a ship which is already authorized to fly the flag of another state, except pursuant to arrangements for transferring the ship
from one state's registry to another. 1958 Convention on the High Seas, Article 6(1); LOS
Convention, Article 92(1).

When Honduras enacted a law providing that a vessel in the service of an individual residing in Honduras would be considered as Honduran, the United States protested that the imposition of Honduran nationality upon a ship flying the United States flag would violate this international principle, and consequently, Honduras did not enforce the law. [1909] U.S. Foreign Relations 367–75. See also 46 U.S.C. § 65b, which makes only those ships not registered under the laws of a foreign nation eligible for United States documentation.

### 3. *Genuine Link*

A second limitation upon the prerogative of a state to confer its nationality on ships is the requirement of a "genuine link" between a ship and its flag state. 1958 Convention on the High Seas, Article 5(1); LOS Convention, Article 91(1). The principle of a genuine link arises from the long-standing practice of states to confer nationality on a ship only upon certain conditions which reflect a connection between the flag state and its ships. These conditions vary among nations, but often include one or more of the following criteria: (1) ownership by nationals, (2) national officers, (3) national crew, and (4) national build. For a summary of various nations' manning and ownership requirements, see Report by the UNCTAD Secretariat, "Conditions for Registration of Ships," U.N. Doc. TD/B/AC.34/2 (1982). The requirement of a sufficient connection between a flag state and its ships is premised upon the belief that a state can carry out its obligation to exercise effective control over its ships only if such a link exists.

After the Second World War, many shipowners tranferred their ships to the registries of countries such as Panama, Liberia, and Honduras in order to avoid increasingly restrictive (and costly) national laws regulating labor and wages, technical and safety standards, pollution control, and other similar matters. For a detailed history of the flight from national flags to "flag of convenience" registries, see Boczek, Flags of Convenience 26–63 (1962). The new host countries did not impose the requirements of national ownership or control, or of national crews or officers, or national build, and permitted easy access to and transfer from their shipping registries, upon payment of modest fees and taxes.

In view of this rise in the use of "flags of convenience," the 1958 Convention on the High Seas incorporated the "genuine link" requirement into Article 5(1), which provision also appears in Article 91(1) of the LOS Convention. The terminology was borrowed from the 1955 decision of the International Court of Justice which held that because of the absence of a "genuine link" between an individual claiming Liechtenstein na-

[*6*]

tionality and Liechtenstein, Guatemala could refuse to recognize Liechtenstein's grant of nationality on the individual. The Nottebohm Case (Liechtenstein v. Guatemala), 1955 I.C.J. 4.

The delegates to the First United Nations Conference on the Law of the Sea (UNCLOS I) refrained from defining genuine link, though early drafts of the International Law Commission had attempted to do so (relying primarily on the criteria of national ownership and national officers). See U.N.Doc. A/CN.4/42 (1951); [1951] 1 Y.B. Int'l L. Comm'n 330–32. The delegates also eliminated a provision which would have enabled states other than the flag state to withhold recognition of a ship's nationality if they considered that there existed no genuine link between the state and the ship. 9 Whiteman, Digest of International Law 14–15 (1968). Article 94(6) of the LOS Convention provides merely that a state "which has clear grounds to believe that proper jurisdiction and control with respect to a ship have not been exercised may report the facts to the flag State," which then has an obligation to investigate the matter.

In 1981, UNCTAD's Committee on Shipping adopted a resolution recommending that "the present régime of open registries [the new name for "flags of convenience"] be gradually transformed into one of normal registries by a process of tightening the conditions under which open-registry countries retain or accept vessels on their registers." U.N. Doc. TD/B/C.4(S–III)/Misc.2 (1981). The developed countries objected to this resolution as an intrusion upon the sovereign right of every state to determine its own registration requirements, although they acknowledged that this right was subject to various obligations, especially with respect to the safety of ships and the protection of the marine environment. U.N. Doc. TD/B/904, at 5–6 (1982).

## C.  DOCUMENTATION AND REGISTRATION

Each state that authorizes a ship to fly its flag must maintain a register of ships containing the name and description of each ship so authorized. The state must also issue documents to ships verifying such authorization. 1958 Convention on the High Seas, Article 5(2); LOS Convention, Article 91(2). The flag symbolizes the nationality of a ship, but in the event that there is a discrepancy between a ship's flag and its documents, the documents control the question of nationality. In The Merritt, 84 U.S. (17 Wall.) 582, 586 (1873), the U.S. Supreme Court stated that "[t]he documents a vessel carries furnish the only evidence of her nationality." Section 65g of Title 46, U.S.C., provides that a certificate of documentation issued under United States shipping laws is "conclusive evidence of nationality for international purposes, but not in any proceeding conducted under the laws of the United States," nor is it conclusive "in any proceeding in which ownership is in issue."

A ship may not change its flag during voyage or while in a port of call unless pursuant to a real change in registry or transfer of ownership. 1958 Convention on the High Seas, Article 6(1); LOS Convention, Article 92(1). The Shipping Act of 1916, 46 U.S.C. § 808, makes a transfer from a United States registry unlawful, unless approved in advance by the Secretary of Transportation. Approval "may be accorded either absolutely or upon such conditions as the Secretary of Transportation prescribes." 46 U.S.C. § 839. At one time, transfer was freely permitted if the new shipowner contracted to make the ship available to the United States in a time of emergency. 46 C.F.R. § 221.13 (1958).

A state can give a temporary authorization for a ship to fly its flag, which often occurs to permit ships purchased abroad to be delivered to the purchaser's country. In certain other exceptional cases, such as where enemy character is at issue or where a ship is in peril, a state may issue a temporary flag even though the ship is entitled to fly the flag of another state. See Rienow, Nationality of a Merchant Vessel 146–49 (1957).

Where a ship's owner fraudulently obtains registration of a ship, the vessel may be liable to

[9]

seizure and forfeiture by the flag state. See, for example, 46 U.S.C. § 65n.

The Vessel Documentation Act of 1980 was enacted to revise and improve United States laws relating to the documentation of vessels. Under 46 U.S.C. § 65b, any vessel of at least five tons that is not registered under the laws of a foreign country is eligible for documentation if it is owned by (1) an individual United States citizen, (2) a partnership whose general partners are United States citizens and whose controlling interest is owned by United States citizens, (3) a United States corporation whose controlling interest is held by United States citizens and whose president and chairman are United States citizens and no more of its directors are noncitizens than a minority of the number necessary to constitute a quorum, or (4) the government (federal, state, or local). See Drzal & Carnilla, "Documentation of Vessels: The Fog Lifts," 13 J.Mar.L. & Com. 261 (1982).

A United States vessel is documented in a designated port of documentation, which is deemed the vessel's home port. 46 U.S.C. §§ 65a, 65c. All vessels eligible for documentation are issued a certificate of documentation, which is endorsed to reflect the various activities in which the vessel may engage. These endorsements include: (1) a registry (which limits a vessel to foreign trade), (2) a coastwise license (which is an all-purpose domestic license encompassing fisheries), (3) a Great Lakes license, (4) a fishery license, and (5) a pleasure vessel license. 46 U.S.C. §§ 65h–65*l*. Only those vessels which are built in the United States may receive a coastwise, Great Lakes, or fishery license.

In the case of a vessel owned by a corporation, association, or partnership, to obtain a coastwise license 75 percent of the interest of such entity must be held by United States citizens. 46 U.S.C. § 802.

Under 46 U.S.C. § 65m, all vessels documented by the United States, whether registered or licensed, must be placed under the command of a United States citizen. In addition, the Merchant Marine Act of 1936 requires that all officers of vessels documented under United States laws be United States citizens. 46 U.S.C. § 1132. If a United States cargo or passenger vessel has received a construction or operation subsidy, the entire crew must be United States citizens. Id. Otherwise, 75 percent of the crew of a United States vessel must be United States citizens.

A vessel documented under United States law which ceases to meet any of the above noted requirements does not automatically regain status as a "vessel of the United States" upon a resumption of the necessary requirements. For example, a United States vessel placed under the command of a foreign citizen must go through the documentation process anew upon resumption of command by a United States citizen. [1978] Digest of U.S. Practice in International Law 970–71. However, automatic reinstatement of status as a United States vessel does occur under some circumstances, such as where a foreign officer fills a vacancy of an officer other than a master while on a foreign voyage and such vacancy is later filled by a United States citizen. 46 U.S.C. § 221.

## D.  SHIPS OR VESSELS

For purposes of the LOS Convention, numerous national laws and international agreements, and as used in this text, the terms "ship" and "vessel" have equivalent meanings, though in some cases attempts have been made to establish a difference between them. Both have been defined in a variety of ways. Early definitions excluded vessels which were not capable of self-propulsion. 1 Gidel, Le Droit International Public de la Mer 70 (1932). The definition of "ship" adopted in the 1962 amendments to the 1954 Oil Pollution Prevention Convention, Article 1(1), limits the meaning of "ship" to "seagoing vessel[s]" actually in the process of "making a sea voyage." Similarly, the 1973 Convention for the Prevention of Pollution from Ships, Article 2(4), defines a "ship" as "a vessel of any type whatsoever operating in the marine environment" and as including "hydrofoil boats, air-cushion vehicles, submersibles, floating craft and fixed or floating platforms." The 1969 Convention on Intervention on the High Seas, Article 2(2)(b), expressly excludes "an installation or device engaged in the exploration and exploitation of the resources of the sea-bed and the ocean floor and subsoil thereof." The U.S. Deepwater Port Act of 1974 defines "vessel" as "every description of watercraft or other artificial contrivance used as a means of transportation on or through water." 33 U.S.C. § 1502(19). Section 801 of Title 46, U.S.C., defines "vessel" to include "all water craft and other artificial contrivances of whatever description and at whatever stage of construction, whether on the stocks or launched, which are used or are capable of being or are intended to be used as a means of transportation on water."

As illustrated above, the term "ship" is defined differently under international and domestic laws, according to the purposes of the instrument defining the term. No single definition of ship exists for all purposes. In Barger v. Petroleum Helicopters, Inc., 514 F.Supp. 1199 (E.D.Tex. 1981), the court found that a helicopter equipped with pontoons and engaged in transporting workers to and from off-shore drilling ships fell within the meaning of vessel for purposes of the Jones Act. Depending upon the legislation involved, oil drilling platforms and similar fixed installations have and have not been held to fall within the meaning of ship.  In In re Complaint of Sedco, Inc., 21 I.L.M. 318, 334–39 (S.D.Tex. 1982), a semisubmersible drilling rig was found to be a vessel for purposes of invoking the Limitation of Liabilities Act, 46 U.S.C. §§ 183 et seq.

# CHAPTER II

## DUTIES AND JURISDICTION OF FLAG STATE AND RESTRICTIONS ON JURISDICTION OF STATES OVER FOREIGN VESSELS

### A.  DUTIES OF FLAG STATE

Each state has a duty under international law to "effectively exercise its jurisdiction and control in administrative, technical and social matters over ships flying its flag."  1958 Convention on the High Seas, Article 5(1).  Article 94 of the LOS Convention further specifies that each flag state has the obligation to:

(1)  Maintain a register of ships authorized to fly its flag;

(2)  Govern the internal affairs of the ship;

(3)  Ensure safety at sea with regard to the construction, equipment and seaworthiness of ships, labor conditions and the training of crews, the maintenance of communications, and the prevention of collisions;

[*15*]

(4) Ensure that each ship is surveyed by a qualified surveyor of ships and has on board appropriate charts, nautical publications, and navigational equipment;

(5) Ensure that each ship is manned by a qualified master, officers and crew; and

(6) Ensure that the master, officers, and, to the appropriate extent, the crew are fully conversant with and are required to observe applicable international regulations regarding the safety of life at sea, the prevention of collisions, the prevention, reduction, and control of marine pollution, and the maintenance of radio communications.

Legislation enacted in fulfilling these obligations must conform to generally accepted international regulations, procedures and practices. The United States, in addition to entering numerous international conventions, has enacted several statutes and regulations to meet its international obligations. Most are found in Title 46 (Shipping) and include, among other matters, the regulation of pilots and pilotage, 46 U.S.C. §§ 211–216; load lines for United States vessels, 46 U.S.C. §§ 86–88i; qualifications of officers and crews of vessels, 46 U.S.C. §§ 221–249c, 46 C.F.R. § 157; wages of masters and seamen, 46 U.S.C. §§ 591–608; carriage of dangerous goods, 46 U.S.C. § 170, 46 C.F.R. § 146; wrecks and salvage, 46 U.S.C. §§ 721–738d;  and ocean dumping, 33 U.S.C. §§ 1401–1444.

The International Maritime Organization (IMO), formerly Inter-Governmental Maritime Consultative Organization (IMCO), and other international bodies have drafted numerous conventions in recent years regarding safety at sea, prevention of collisions, pollution control, maritime traffic, maritime communications, and related matters.  Many of these conventions have become "generally accepted" and therefore are applicable to all states, even those not ratifying a particular convention.  Among these conventions are the 1910 Assistance and Salvage at Sea Convention, the 1960 and 1974 Safety of Life at Sea Conventions, the 1954 Oil Prevention Pollution Convention, the 1965 Maritime Traffic Convention, the 1972 Convention on Preventing Collisions at Sea, and the 1966 Load Lines Convention.

# B.  JURISDICTION OF FLAG STATE AND RESTRICTIONS ON JURISDICTION OF STATES OVER FOREIGN VESSELS

## 1.  *High Seas*

The flag state has exclusive jurisdiction over its ships on the high seas, except where expressly provided otherwise by international agreement. 1958 Convention on the High Seas, Article 6(1); LOS Convention, Article 92(1).  Though the no-tion that a ship is a floating part of the flag state is generally recognized as fiction, the law of the flag state is applied "on the pragmatic basis that there must be some law on shipboard, that it cannot change at every change of waters, and no experience shows a better rule than that of the state that owns her." Lauritzen v. Larsen, 345 U.S. 571, 585 (1953). However, the U. S. Supreme Court has also noted that a flag state's jurisdiction over a vessel "partakes more of the characteristics of personal than of territorial sovereignty," and on this basis refused to apply the National Prohibition Act to United States ships outside of United States territorial waters. Cunard S.S. Co. v. Mellon, 262 U.S. 100, 123 (1923). Similarly, in Lam Mow v. Nagle, 24 F.2d 316 (9th Cir. 1928), the court held that a person born aboard a United States ship was not born in the United States and not entitled to United States citizenship.

Where conduct occurring on a ship on the high seas produces an effect on a foreign vessel or in foreign territory, the laws of each ship concerned may be applied. In The S.S. Lotus, P.C.I.J. Ser. A, No. 10 (1927), a French and Turkish vessel collided on the high seas. France argued that it alone had jurisdiction over the conduct occurring on the French vessel on the high seas, but the Permanent Court held that Turkey could instigate a criminal proceeding against the French officer because the effect of his offense was felt by the Turkish vessel. This rule has been changed by several international agreements, which limit jurisdiction to the flag state of the vessel alleged to be responsible for the collision and the state of nationality of the accused, in order to avoid delays in maritime transport which would otherwise arise. See, for example, the 1952 Convention on Penal Jurisdiction in Matters of Collision; 1958 Convention on the High Seas, Article 11; LOS Convention, Article 97.

Where provided for by treaty, or when consented to by the flag state, a vessel on the high seas may be boarded and searched (and sometimes seized) by a government ship of a foreign state. In United States v. Green, 671 F.2d 46, 50 (1st Cir. 1982), the Court stated that "[g]iven this waiver [of the flag state], the individuals on board cannot successfully argue that [the 1958 Convention on the High Seas] was violated." The most common arrangements for such cooperation relate to the prevention of piracy, slave trade, illicit drug traffic, and unauthorized broadcasting on the high seas. See, for example, 1958 Convention on the High Seas, Article 13–22; LOS Convention, Articles 99–110; 1980 United States-Colombia Narcotics Agreement; 1974 United States-Jamaica Narcotics Agreement.

A ship engaged in piracy on the high seas may be seized by any state, but where such a seizure has been effected without adequate grounds, the seizing state shall be liable for damages to the flag state. 1958 Convention on the High Seas, Articles 19–21; LOS Convention, Articles 105–107. In case of unauthorized broadcasting, seizure of a ship is permitted under Article 109(4) of the LOS Convention.

Under the 1958 Convention on the High Seas, Article 13, and the LOS Convention, Articles 99, 108, and 110, seizure is not an available remedy for the prevention of slave trade or illicit drug traffic, unless specially provided for by treaty. In Le Louis, 2 Dods. 210 (1817), a British government vessel seized a French ship on the high seas, alleging that the French ship was engaged in the slave trade and subject to seizure under international law. Sir William Scott (later Lord Stowell) held that the British ship was not justified in seizing the French ship under international law at that time. Chief Justice Marshall came to the same conclusion. The Antelope, 23 U.S. (10 Wheat.) 66, 116–25 (1825). But see Justice Story's decision in United States v. The Schooner La Jeune Eugenie, 26 Fed.Case No. 15,551, 2 Mason (U.S. Cir.Ct.Mass.) 409 (1822). Recent conventions against slavery, such as the 1926 Slavery Convention, do not contain any specific right of enforcement against non-nationals on the high seas. But see 1958 Convention on the High Seas, Article 22; LOS Convention, Article 110 (boarding and verification of the right to fly the flag allowed, but not seizure).

When there is reasonable ground for suspecting that a foreign ship is engaged in unauthorized broadcasting, the ship may be boarded by a warship of a state having jurisdiction over that illegal activity. LOS Convention, Article 110(1)(c). Such jurisdiction may be exercised by a court of the flag state (or state of registry if an installation), the state of which the person engaged in unauthorized broadcasting is a national, any state where the transmissions can be received, or any state where authorized radio communication is suffering interference. Id., Article 109(3).

All states are under a duty to cooperate for the suppression of illicit drug traffic. Id., Article 108; 1961 Single Convention on Narcotic Drugs, Article 35. Neither of these Conventions authorizes the boarding, searching or seizure of a foreign flag vessel suspected of engaging in illicit drug trade.

Another exception which justifies interference by a government ship of a foreign ship on the high seas is where the government ship has reason to suspect that, though flying a foreign flag, the ship has the same nationality as the government ship. 1958 Convention on the High Seas, Article 22(1)(e); LOS Convention, Article 110 (1)(e). In United States v. Ricardo, 619 F.2d 1124, 1130 n. 4 (5th Cir. 1980), the court stated that "[f]ailure to fly its flag or exhibit its nationality, the presence of American interpreters, and the proximity to and bearing towards the United States coast generate ample suspicion that the [ship] may have been of American registry."

A stateless ship and a ship flying under more than one flag at its convenience are not entitled to protection against boarding and search on the high seas. 1958 Convention on the High Seas, Article 6(2); LOS Convention, Article 92(2). The Marijuana on the High Seas Act, 21 U.S.C. § 955b(d), expressly extends jurisdiction to vessels "without nationality or a vessel assimilated to a vessel without nationality," in accordance with Article 6(2) of the 1958 Convention on the High Seas. In United States v. Marino-Garcia, 679 F. 2d 1373 (11th Cir. 1982), the court upheld the legality under international law of the search of a vessel which claimed two nationalities, and the extension of United States jurisdiction under the Marijuana on the High Seas Act, 21 U.S.C. § 955a, to the non-national crew and officers of the vessel even in the absence of evidence that the illicit drugs discovered on board were intended for distribution in the United States. The court denied that a nexus between the vessel assimilated to statelessness and the country seeking jurisdiction was necessary, stating that "[j]urisdiction exists *solely* as a consequence of the vessel's status as stateless." United States v. Marino-Garcia, supra, at 1383.

Another exception to the exclusive right of a flag state to exercise jurisdiction over its ships on the high seas is the "right of hot pursuit." A coastal state may engage in pursuit of a foreign ship beyond its territorial waters and contiguous zone if the state has reason to believe the ship has violated its laws. The right of hot pursuit ceases as soon as the ship pursued enters the territorial waters of another state. 1958 Convention on the High Seas, Article 23; LOS Convention, Article 111.

### 2. U.S. Practice Concerning Search and Seizure on the High Seas

Under 14 U.S.C. § 89, the United States Coast Guard may search, seize and arrest "any vessel subject to the jurisdiction, or to the operation of any law, of the United States" in order to prevent, detect or suppress violations of United States laws. Under 19 U.S.C. § 1581(a), customs officers (including the Coast Guard) may, within the customs waters or customs enforcement areas of the United States, "go on board of any vessel . . . and examine, inspect, and search the vessel" without regard to its nationality for purposes of enforcing United States customs laws. If a violation is discovered, the ship may be seized.

Treasury regulation 19 C.F.R. § 162.3 provides that a customs officer may board "any American vessel on the high seas" to examine, inspect, and search the vessel "when there is probable cause to believe that such vessel is violating or has violated the laws of the United States." The regulation does not require probable cause to board any vessel within United States waters. Foreign vessels may not be boarded on the high seas "in contravention of any treaty with a foreign government."

The Supreme Court has acknowledged the authority of United States officials to search and seize a United States vessel on the high seas upon a showing of probable cause. United States v. Lee, 274 U.S. 559 (1927). In the early 1970's, the United States Coast Guard engaged in an active campaign against drug smuggling into the United States from the Caribbean. Many of its activities in boarding, searching, and arresting vessels and their occupants outside of United States territorial waters were challenged, primarily in the Fifth Circuit, for lack of probable cause. Divergent opinions within the Fifth Circuit and among other circuits have arisen regarding whether the Fourth and Fifth Amendments are applicable to vessel searches and, if so, under what standards. One line of cases has taken the position that 14 U.S.C. § 89 empowers the Coast Guard to seize and board vessels of the United States flag on the high seas without probable cause or any other particularized suspicion. See, e.g., United States v. Warren, 578 F.2d 1058 (5th Cir. 1978). Another line of cases takes the position that the Fourth and Fifth Amendments are applicable to high sea searches and seizures under the same standards as those applied to territorial searches and seizures. United States v. Streifel, 665 F.2d 414 (2d Cir. 1981) (requiring reasonable suspicion to search Panamanian vessel on the high seas even after having obtained the consent of the Panamanian government to board). See also United States v. Piner, 608 F.2d 358 (9th Cir. 1979) (random stop and safety inspection of United States vessel in territorial waters by Coast Guard without reasonable suspicion of noncompliance with safety laws violates Fourth Amendment).

Confusion has also arisen in the Fifth Circuit and others regarding the applicability of 14 U.S. C. § 89 to foreign vessels on the high seas by virtue of the language extending jurisdiction over any vessel "subject . . . to the operation of any law, of the United States." In United States v. Cadena, 585 F.2d 1252 (5th Cir. 1978), the court interpreted this language to extend jurisdiction over crimes committed on a foreign vessel which would have an impact in the territory of the United States (such as drug smuggling). The court assumed, arguendo, that such an interpretation would result in a violation of Article 6 of the 1958 Convention on the High Seas, but held that a treaty violation was insufficient grounds to dismiss jurisdiction or suppress evidence where the defendants were nationals of states who were not signatories to the treaty.

In United States v. Postal, 589 F.2d 862 (5th Cir. 1979), defendants (nationals of countries which had signed the 1958 Convention on the High Seas) contended that the court had no jurisdiction over them because the boarding and arrest by the Coast Guard of foreign crew members on a foreign ship on the high seas violated the United States obligations under the 1958 Convention on the High Seas. The defendants relied on Cook v. United States, 288 U.S. 102 (1933), which held that the Ker-Frisbie doctrine (under which a defendant may not assert the illegality of his detention to defeat jurisdiction over him) is inapplicable where the illegality results from a treaty violation. The court in Postal interpreted Cook to apply only where a self-executing treaty is involved, and proceeded to find the Convention on the High Seas non-self-executing and therefore applied the Ker-Frisbie doctrine to uphold jurisdiction.

To clarify and broaden United States jurisdiction over narcotics smuggling, Congress enacted in 1980 the Marijuana on the High Seas Act, 21

U.S.C. §§ 955a–955d, which asserts jurisdiction over:

(a) any vessel documented under United States laws;

(b) any vessel owned in whole or in part by a United States citizen or corporation, unless such vessel has been granted nationality by a foreign nation; and

(c) any vessel without nationality or a vessel assimilated to statelessness under Article 6(2) of the Convention on the High Seas.

Doubts have been expressed with respect to the consistency of this Act with international law. See Note, "High Seas Narcotics Smuggling and Section 955a and Title 21: Overextension of the Protective Principle of International Jurisdiction," 50 Fordham L.Rev. 688 (1982).

*3. Contiguous Zone*

In a zone contiguous to its territorial sea, a coastal state may exercise its jurisdiction over foreign vessels to the extent necessary to prevent infringement of its customs, fiscal, immigration or sanitary laws and regulations within its territory or territorial sea. 1958 Territorial Sea Convention, Article 24(1); LOS Convention, Article 33(1). See the discussion in Chapter VI, Section G.

## 4. Exclusive Economic Zone

A coastal state has limited jurisdiction over foreign vessels within its exclusive economic zone with regard to the exercise and enforcement of its rights to explore, exploit, conserve and manage the living resources of the exclusive economic zone. See the discussion in Chapter VII, particularly Section E.

## 5. Territorial Waters

A coastal state may exercise limited civil and criminal jurisdiction over foreign vessels passing through its territorial sea. Chapter VI discusses in detail coastal state jurisdiction in its territorial water.

## 6. Internal Waters and Ports

The restrictions on a coastal state's jurisdiction diminish when a foreign ship enters its internal waters and ports. For a detailed discussion of the scope of a coastal state's jurisdiction over foreign ships in its internal waters and ports, see Chapter V, Section C.

## 7. Jurisdiction over Ships Owned by Nationals

A state has jurisdiction for certain purposes over ships owned by nationals, although such ships fly the flag of another state. The United States Criminal Code, 18 U.S.C. § 7(1), extends criminal jurisdiction to acts committed on "any vessel belonging in whole or in part to the United States or any citizen thereof . . . when such vessel is within the admiralty and maritime jurisdiction of the United States." In United States v. Plumer, 27 Fed.Case No. 16,056 (1859), the court interpreted this "special maritime jurisdiction" not to extend United States criminal jurisdiction over "a foreign vessel, except to a very limited extent, and never where the perpetrator of the crime, and the deceased, were both foreigners." The "very limited" exception applies where "the vessel [is] sailing under no national flag." Id. at 575. In United States v. Keller, 451 F.Supp. 631, 636–37 (D. Puerto Rico 1978), the court applied this statute to uphold jurisdiction over foreign crew members arrested on the high seas on board a ship flying no flag which was owned in part by United States citizens and thus subject to the special maritime jurisdiction. However, the court stated that an additional basis of jurisdiction was that the ship was entitled to fly the United States flag. Id. at 637 n. 9.

The High Seas Gambling Act, 18 U.S.C. §§ 1081–1083, prohibits gambling upon United States vessels. The term "American vessel" is defined for purposes of the Act to include "any vessel which is neither documented . . . under the laws of the United States nor documented under the laws of any foreign country, if such vessel is owned by, chartered to, or otherwise controlled by one or more citizens or residents of the United States or corporations organized under the laws of the United States or of any [United States] State."

For purposes of the Marijuana on the High Seas Act, 21 U.S.C. § 955b, a "vessel of the United States" includes any vessel "owned in whole or in part by the United States or a citizen of the United States" or a United States corporation, unless the vessel has been granted nationality by a foreign nation.

Section 902 of the Merchant Marine Act, 46 U.S.C. § 1242, authorizes the United States to requisition any vessel owned by a United States citizen, including corporations, during an emergency declared by presidential proclamation, in return for just compensation.  During the First World War, Great Britain attempted to requisition Dutch-registered vessels indirectly owned by British nationals.  The British government initially based its rights on the necessity of protecting the interests of its nationals, but later based its rights on national security.  The Netherlands protested, stating that only the flag state has the right to requisition its ships, whereupon Great Britain refrained from carrying out the requisition.  See Boczek, Flags of Convenience 196–97 (1962).  With regard to Britain's first claim that a state has the right to protect the interests of its citizens in a foreign vessel, see Watts, "The Protection of Merchant Ships," 33 Brit.Y.B.Int'l L. 52 (1957).

During a national emergency proclaimed by the President, it is unlawful to transfer to a foreign registry or to sell, mortgage or lease any vessel owned in whole or in part by a United States citizen or corporation without prior approval. 46 U.S.C. § 835.

In the time of war, numerous prize courts have upheld the condemnation of a vessel registered in a neutral state but owned by nationals of an enemy state. However, determination that a ship has an enemy character and therefore is subject to condemnation does not mean that the condemned ship bears the nationality of the enemy state. See Rienow, Nationality of a Merchant Vessel 117–39 (1937).

## 8.   *Government Vessels*

Warships and government vessels used for noncommercial service on the high seas have complete immunity from interference by states other than the flag state. 1958 Convention on the High Seas, Article 9; LOS Convention, Articles 95–96. While a foreign warship or government noncommercial ship is in the territorial or internal waters of a coastal state, the coastal state cannot extend its criminal jurisdiction over such ships. In The Schooner Exchange v. McFadden, 11 U.S. (7 Cranch) 116 (1812), plaintiffs commenced proceedings to obtain possession of a ship previously owned by them which had been seized by the French government and converted into a French warship while the ship was in a   United States port.   The Supreme Court deferred to the "principle of public law, that national ships of war, entering the port of a friendly power open for their reception, are to be considered as exempted by the consent of that power from its jurisdiction."   Id. at 145–46.

A foreign warship or government noncommercial vessel which enters the territorial or internal waters of a coastal state must adhere to the laws and regulations governing passage through the territorial sea and admission into a port.   A war ship or government noncommercial vessel not complying with such laws may be requested or required to leave coastal state waters.   1958 Territorial Sea Convention, Article 23;  LOS Convention, Article 30.   A coastal state can levy charges for specific services rendered to a foreign government ship.   LOS Convention, Article 26(2).

Governments have increasingly used government vessels for the purposes of engaging in trade.   In Berizzi Brothers Co. v. The S.S. Pesaro, 271 U.S. 562, 574 (1926), the Supreme Court held that government commercial ships "must be held to have the same immunity as war ships."   In Mexico v. Hoffman, 324 U.S. 30 (1945), the Supreme Court denied, however, immunity from jurisdiction to a commercial ship owned but not possessed by the Mexican government.

The United States Department of State adopted in 1952 a policy of not claiming immunity in claims against government owned or operated commercial ships. 26 Dep't State Bull. 984 (1952). The Foreign Sovereign Immunity Act of 1976, 28 U.S.C. §§ 1602 et seq., provides that a foreign state shall not be immune from United States jurisdiction in any case "in which the action is based upon a commercial activity carried on . . . by the foreign state." The commercial activity must occur in the United States or waters over which it has jursdiction or have a direct effect in the United States. 28 U.S.C. § 1605(a)(2). The Act also provides that a foreign state is not immune from jurisdiction in any case against a foreign government commercial ship to enforce a maritime lien. Id., § 1605(b). For cases applying this Act, see Valenti, "The Use of Procedure to Effect Equity: Section 1605 (b) of the Foreign Sovereign Immunities Act of 1976," 10 Fla.St.U.L.Rev. 129, 135–47 (1982); Perez v. Bahamas, 652 F.2d 186 (D.C.Cir. 1981); Complaint of Rio Grande Transport, Inc., 516 F. Supp. 1155 (S.D.N.Y.1981); China National Chemical Import & Export Corp. v. M/V Lago Hualaihue, 504 F.Supp. 684 (D.C.Md.1981).

For a collection of national laws regulating foreign government warships in the territorial

[*33*]

sea, see, e.g., National Legislation and Treaties Relating to the Law of the Sea, U.N. Doc. ST/LEG/SER. B/19 at 149 (1978).

## 9.   *Special United States Statutes*

The Death on the High Seas Act of 1920, 46 U.S.C. §§ 761–768, provides for recovery in United States courts for any deaths "caused by wrongful act, neglect, or default occurring on the high seas." The Jones Act of 1920 provides that any seaman who is injured or dies in the course of his employment may maintain an action for damages in United States courts.   46 U.S.C. § 688.

Read literally, these two acts permit any party injured on the high seas recourse in United States courts, regardless of the nationality of the party or the ship or shipowner involved.   The Supreme Court has limited the applicability of the statutes "only to areas and transactions in which American law would be considered operative under prevalent doctrines of international law." Lauritzen v. Larsen, 345 U.S. 571, 577 (1953).

The relevant considerations in determining the applicability of the Jones Act are (1) the place of the wrongful act, (2) the law of the flag state, (3) the allegiance or domicile of the injured party, (4) the allegiance of the defendant, (5) the place of contract, (6) the inaccessibility of a foreign forum, (7) the law of the forum and (8) the location of the defendant's base of operations.

[*34*]

Id. at 582–89; Hellenic Lines v. Rhoditis, 398 U.S. 306, 309 (1970). Heavy weight must be given to the law of the flag state, though this factor is not conclusive. In Lauritzen, applicability of the Jones Act was denied in an action brought by a foreign seaman injured on a foreign ship in the territorial waters of a foreign state. In Rhoditis, the Jones Act was held applicable where a foreign national injured in a United States port aboard a foreign vessel brought suit against a foreign employer residing in the United States whose base of shipping operations was the United States. Even where sufficient contacts exist, a United States court may decline jurisdiction on the principle of forum non conveniens. See Bickel, "The Doctrine of Forum Non Conveniens as Applied in the Federal Court in Matters of Admiralty." 35 Corn.L.Q. 12 (1949).

# CHAPTER III

# THE BASELINE FOR DETERMINING ZONES OF NATIONAL JURISDICTION

## A. INTRODUCTION

There are three types of delimitations involved in determining the zones of a coastal state's maritime jurisdiction. This chapter addresses the first delimitation—the "baseline" from which the breadth of a coastal state's various maritime jurisdictions is measured. The second type of delimitation determines the outer limit of each zone of maritime jurisdiction; it is discussed in Chapters VI–VIII. The final type of delimitation, discussed in Chapter IV, determines the boundaries of maritime jurisdiction between states with adjacent or opposite coasts.

It is a well-established principle of international law that although the determination of a boundary by a state is often a unilateral act, its validity with regard to other states depends upon international law. The International Court of Justice acknowledged the applicability of this principle to maritime boundaries in the Fisheries Case (U. K.

v. Norway), stating that "[t]he delimitation of the sea areas has always an international aspect; it cannot be dependent merely upon the will of

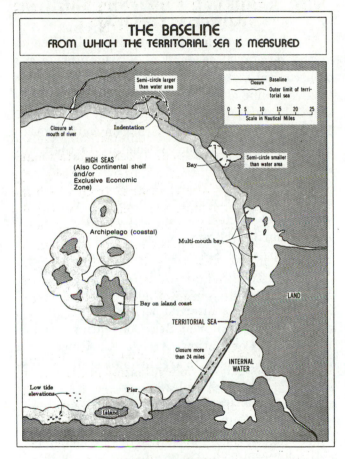

**Illustration 1**

[*37*]

the coastal State as expressed in its municipal
law." 1951 I.C.J. 116, 132.

## B.  NORMAL BASELINE: THE LOW–WATER LINE

The normal baseline for measuring the breadth
of the territorial sea and of all the other zones
of a coastal state's maritime jurisdiction is "the
low-water line along the coast as marked on large-
scale charts officially recognized by the coastal
State." 1958 Territorial Sea Convention, Article 3; LOS Convention, Article 5. In the many
geographical circumstances where internal waters
(such as bays) border a coastal state's territorial
sea, the line of demarcation between the internal
waters and the territorial sea forms the baseline
for measuring the zones of maritime jurisdiction.
1958 Territorial Sea Convention, Articles 7 and
13; LOS Convention, Articles 9–10.

Waters on the landward side of the baseline
form part of the internal waters of the coastal
state. 1958 Territorial Sea Convention, Article
5(1); LOS Convention, Article 8. However, a
different rule applies to archipelagic states, as discussed in Section I, infra.

In the Fisheries Case (U. K. v. Norway), the
International Court found that "for the purpose of
measuring the breadth of the territorial sea, it
is the low-water mark as opposed to the high-
water mark, or the mean between the two tides,

[*38*]

which has generally been adopted in the practice of States. This criterion is the most favorable to the coastal State and clearly shows the character of territorial waters as appurtenant to the land territory." 1951 I.C.J. 116, 128.

"Low-water marks" are not constant; they shift from day to day and season to season. For a discussion of the many geographical methods of determining low-water lines, see Boggs, "Delimitation of Seaward Areas under National Jurisdiction," 45 A.J.I.L. 240, 244–45, 251–54 (1951). Neither the 1958 Territorial Sea Convention nor the LOS Convention prescribes the methods to be used by coastal states in determining the low-water mark. A state may employ any method available, but must publish the low-water lines on officially recognized, large-scale charts so that navigators will be aware of the methods used.

In United States v. California, the United States asserted that the low-water line is determined by averaging all of the low tides; California asserted that only the lower low tides are to be taken into account. The Court agreed with the latter view, noting that only the lower low-water line was marked on the U.S. Coast and Geodetic Survey's charts. 381 U.S. 139, 175–76 (1956).

## C.  RIVERS

Where a river flows directly into the sea, the baseline is a straight line across the mouth of the river between points on the low-water line of its banks. 1958 Territorial Sea Convention, Article 13; LOS Convention, Article 9. The 1956 draft of the International Law Commission provided a special rule where a river flows into an estuary, in which case the rules governing bays were to apply. [1956] 2 Y.B. Int'l L.Comm'n 253, 271–72. Though the provision was not incorporated into the 1958 Convention, the United States has adopted this principle and on this basis objected along with the United Kingdom and the Netherlands to the use of a straight line in 1961 by Argentina and Uruguay across the mouth of the Rio de la Plata in fixing the baseline from which to measure maritime zones. 4 Whiteman, Digest of International Law 339–43 (1965). See also the recommendations of the Special Master noted in United States v. California, which adopt this rule. 381 U.S. 139, 144–45 n. 6 (1965).

Where a river forms a delta at its entrance to the sea which is highly unstable, the coastal state may draw straight lines from appropriate points across the most seaward low-water lines of the delta. The baselines so drawn shall remain effective in spite of subsequent regressions of the delta until changed by the coastal state in accordance with the LOS Convention. LOS Convention, Article 7(2). This provision was incorporated to protect the interests of deltaic countries such as Bangladesh whose shorelines are characterized by continual fluvial erosion and sedimentation. [1978] Digest of U.S. Practice in International Law 942–43. In the United States, this provision may be applicable to the Mississippi delta.

## D. BAYS

The waters of a bay are considered as internal waters of a coastal state if the bay possesses prescribed geographic characteristics. It must be a well-marked indentation in the coast which is more than a mere curvature. This requirement is met when a bay's area is as large as or larger than that of the semi-circle whose diameter is a line drawn across its mouth. The closing line between the natural entrance points of a bay may not exceed 24 nautical miles. Where the closing line does exceed 24 nautical miles, a straight baseline of 24 nautical miles may be drawn within the bay in such a manner as to enclose the maximum area of water that is possible within a line of that length. 1958 Territorial Sea Convention, Article 7; LOS Convention, Article 10.

In addition, international law recognizes "historic" bays that, based upon previous usage, have been considered internal waters even though they do not satisfy the above geographical criteria for a bay. Historic waters, including historic bays, are discussed in Section J, infra.

An early landmark in the development of the law of bays was the North Atlantic Fisheries

Case (Great Britain v. United States), decided by a tribunal of the Permanent Court of Arbitration in 1910, which involved in part the interpretation of the term "bay" as used in the 1818 United States-Great Britain Fisheries Convention. See 1 Scott, The Hague Court Reports 141, 188 (1916). The United States requested the Court to apply a mathematical rule for defining bays, limiting bays to a 6-, 10-, or 12-mile closing line. In defending its position, the United States relied on state practice as evidenced by numerous treaties which provided that the mouth of a bay might be no more than 10 miles wide, such as the 1882 North Sea Fisheries Convention, Article 2(2). The Court held that state practice did not establish a generally applicable mathematical closing rule as a rule of international law. The tribunal adopted a general definition of the term "bay" which relied primarily on geographic factors such as the length of the bay, penetration inland relative to the width of its mouth, the proximity of the bay to the navigational routes of the high seas, and to some extent on such nongeographic factors as defense needs and the economic importance of the enclosed waters to the local population. Id. at 186–88. The International Court of Justice also rejected the 10-mile limit as a rule of international law in the Fisheries Case (U. K. v. Norway), 1951 I.C.J. 116, 131.

Departing from a proposal by the International Law Commission that a closing line of 15 miles be adopted as a compromise between the 10-mile rule and the 24-mile rule supported by states claiming a 12-mile territorial sea ([1956] 2 Y.B. Int'l L. Comm'n 268–69), the 1958 Geneva Conference approved a 24-mile line. 3 UNCLOS I Off. Rec. 144–46 (1958).

The source of the semi-circle rule is the Report of the Committee of Experts on Technical Questions Concerning the Territorial Sea, annexed to U.N. Doc. A/CN.4/61/Add. 1 (1953), [1953] 2 Y.B. Int'l L.Comm'n 75, 77. In applying the semi-circle test, the closing line is drawn between the natural entrance points of the bay. In computing the area, islands within the indentation are included as if they were part of the water area. 1958 Territorial Sea Convention, Article 7(3); LOS Convention, Article 10(3).

In interpreting the Submerged Lands Act of 1953, 43 U.S.C. §§ 1301–1315, in United States v. Louisiana, the Supreme Court applied the 1958 Convention rules regarding the drawing of baselines across bays. 394 U.S. 11 (1969). One question presented to it was "to what extent indentations within or tributary to another indentation can be included in the latter for purposes of the semicircle test." The United States adopted the position that inner indentations be included for the semi-circle test only if they can reasonably be considered part of the single, outer indentation. Indentations separated from another indentation by a line of islands or linked only by narrow passages may not be considered. The Court did include an inner bay separated from a larger bay only by a string of islands across the mouth of the inner bay, but did not include an inner bay which was linked to a larger indentation only by a narrow channel. Id. at 48–51.

A second issue raised was whether the headland for determining the closing line could be situated on an island in close proximity to the mainland at the entrance of the bay. The Court noted that though generally islands are not headlands of a bay but only create multiple mouths, there may be instances where islands are such an integral part of the coast that they may be used as a headland from which the closing line is drawn. Factors such as the island's size, its distance from the shore, its shape, its relationship to the configuration of the coast, and the depth and utility of the intervening waters, determine whether the island constitutes an integral part of the coast. Id. at 66.

Where islands appear in the mouth of a bay, the Court held that the closing line of the bay should be drawn between appropriate points on the low-water lines of the islands. The Court rejected Louisiana's argument that islands present in the mouth of a bay should not be used to draw landward a direct line between the headlands of a bay. Id. at 55–60. For another application of these principles, see United States v. California (Decree), 432 U.S. 40, 41 (1977).

The Supreme Court refused to consider the Santa Barbara Channel as a bay simply because the openings at both ends of the channel and between the islands fringing the seaward side of the channel were all less than 24 miles. United States v. California, 381 U.S. 139, 170–72 (1965).

The headlands for the closing lines of certain bays were held to be "the seaward ends of the jetties located at their mouths." United States v. California, 432 U.S. 40 (1977).

Article 7 of the 1958 Territorial Sea Convention and Article 10 of the LOS Convention do not apply to bays bounded by more than one state. The rule with respect to such bays is not clear. One view is that each state bordering the bay has a belt of territorial waters, and the remainder of the bay is part of the high seas, open to navigation by vessels of third nations. A second view was set forth in El Salvador v. Nicaragua, decided in 1917 by the Central American Court of Justice, 11 A.J.I.L. 674 (1917). In that case, the Court found on the basis of special historic and geographic facts that the Gulf of Fonseca which is bordered by El Salvador and Nicaragua at its headlands and by the Honduras at its base was held, as against the rest of the world, in community by the three states, except for an exclusive territorial belt which each of the three states held off its coast. Id. at 711. Under this theory, one coastal state cannot alter, deliver to or share with another the use and enjoyment of the common waters without the consent of the other states who hold a common interest in the bay waters. The case was decided in the context of the proposed construction of an inter-oceanic canal, and its general applicability is open to considerable question. According to a third view, the bay is divided among the bordering states according to principles applicable to states with adjacent or opposite coasts (see Chapter IV).

## E.  ISLANDS

All islands are entitled to a territorial sea, exclusive economic zone, and continental shelf. An island is "a naturally-formed area of land, surrounded by water, which is above water at high tide." 1958 Territorial Sea Convention, Article 10; LOS Convention, Article 121. By implication, artificial islands or installations are not islands which are entitled to a territorial sea, exclusive economic zone, or continental shelf, nor may they be considered in determining baselines. United States v. California, 447 U.S. 1, 4 n. 3 (1980). However, a coastal state may establish a safety zone around artificial islands or installations in which it may prescribe appropriate

[46]

measures to ensure the safety of navigation and of the artificial islands or installations. LOS Convention, Article 60(4)–(5). See generally Papadakis, The International Legal Regime of Artificial Islands (1977).

Rocks which cannot sustain human habitation or economic life have only a territorial sea. LOS Convention, Article 121.

The presence of an island or a small group of islands in close proximity to the mainland raises the question of whether the baseline should depart from the low-water line of the mainland to encompass such islands, in which case the waters so embraced are internal waters. A distinction must be made between a fringe of islands and the presence of one or a few scattered islands off the coast. Where they are sufficient in number to constitute a fringe of islands which are closely linked to the land, straight baselines can be drawn as discussed in detail at Section H, infra. 1958 Territorial Sea Convention, Article 4; LOS Convention, Article 7; Fisheries Case (U. K. v. Norway), 1951 I.C.J. 116. Where there are islands immediately proximate to the mainland, it has been suggested that in such a case an exception may be made to the normal low-water line baseline, and the coastal state may draw the baseline to encompass such islands. [1953] 2 Y.B. Int'l L.Comm'n 57, 65–66. This proposal was based on a draft prepared by the Second Subcommittee of the Territorial Waters Commission at the 1930 Hague Conference. See Acts of the Conference for the Codification of International Law, L.N. Pub. 1930.V.16 at 206. The Director of the Coast and Geodetic Survey, Department of Commerce, has stated that "[t]he coast line should not depart from the mainland to embrace offshore islands, except where such islands either form a portico to the mainland . . . or they form an integral part of a land form." Memorandum of April 18, 1961, excerpted in 1 Shalowitz, Shore and Sea Boundaries 161 n. 125 (1962).

As early as the case of The Anna, 165 Eng.Rep. 809, 815 (1805), Lord Stowell concluded that "a number of little mud islands composed of earth and trees drifted down" by the Mississippi River, incapable of supporting life "are the natural appendage of the coast on which they border," and therefore served as the baseline from which the limits of the territorial sea were to be measured.

In United States v. Louisiana, 394 U.S. 11, 61–66 (1969), the Supreme Court acknowledged that an island could be assimilated to the mainland for purposes of determining the baselines:

> [T]he question whether a particular island is to be treated as part of the mainland would depend on such factors as its size, its distance from the mainland, the depth and utility of the intervening waters, the shape of the

island, and its relationship to the configuration or curvature of the coast.

Id. at 66.

In Louisiana v. Mississippi, the Supreme Court found that St. Bernard Peninsula, a land formation consisting in large part of uninhabited mud islands, formed an integral part of the coast of Louisiana. 202 U.S. 1, 45–47 (1906). See also United States v. Louisiana, 394 U.S. 11, 62–63 (1969) (the Supreme Court took judicial notice of the fact that the United States claims as a part of the mainland a portion of the Louisiana coast consisting of numerous small mud islands).

## F. LOW–TIDE ELEVATIONS

A low-tide elevation is a naturally formed area of land which is surrounded by and above water at low tide but submerged at high tide. Low-tide elevations situated wholly or partly within a territorial sea may be used as the baseline for measuring the breadth of the territorial sea. Low-tide elevations situated wholly outside of the territorial sea of the mainland or an island have no territorial sea of their own. 1958 Territorial Sea Convention, Article 11; LOS Convention, Article 13.

In United States v. Louisiana, the Supreme Court held that low-tide elevations situated within three miles of bay-closing lines but further than three miles from the mainland constituted a part of the coastline from which the territorial sea is measured. 394 U.S. 11, 40–47 (1969). In the case of islands situated on atolls or of islands having fringing reefs, the baseline is the seaward low-water line of the reef. LOS Convention, Article 6.

## G. HARBORS AND ROADSTEADS

For the purpose of delimiting the territorial sea, the outermost permanent harbor works which form an integral part of the harbor system are regarded as forming part of the coast. Offshore installations and artificial islands are not considered as permanent harbor works. 1958 Territorial Sea Convention, Article 8; LOS Convention, Article 11. The U.S. Supreme Court has stated that "harbor works" connote "structures" and "installations" that were "part of the land," that in some sense enclosed and sheltered the waters within, and that were "connected with the coast." Therefore, "dredged channels leading to ports and harbors" were not "harbor works." United States v. Louisiana, 394 U.S. 11, 36–38 (1969).

In United States v. California, the Supreme Court found certain jetties, breakwaters and other artificial structures as part of the coastline for baseline purposes. 432 U.S. 40, 41–42 (1977). The Supreme Court, however, refused such treatment to piers which were not coast protective works and to an artificial island used to service offshore oil facilities. United States v. California, 447 U.S. 1, 8 (1980).

[*50*]

Roadsteads are places at a distance from the coast that are used for the loading, unloading and anchoring of ships. Roadsteads which are situated wholly or partially outside the outer limit of the territorial sea are included in the territorial sea. 1958 Territorial Sea Convention, Article 9; LOS Convention, Article 12. As they are considered a part of the territorial sea and not of the internal waters, their delimitation does not influence the baseline from which the areas of coastal jurisdiction are measured. See McDougal & Burke, The Public Order of the Oceans 423–37 (1962). Deepwater ports established under the Deepwater Port Act of 1974, 33 U.S.C. §§ 1501 et seq., do not affect the baseline. Concerning these ports, see also Chapter VII, Section I, infra.

## H.  STRAIGHT BASELINES

"In localities where the coastline is deeply indented and cut into, or if there is a fringe of islands along the coast in its immediate vicinity, the method of straight baselines joining appropriate points may be employed in drawing the baseline from which the breadth of the territorial sea is measured." 1958 Territorial Sea Convention, Article 4(1); LOS Convention, Article 7(1). This provision is based on the Fisheries Case (U. K. v. Norway), in which the International Court of Justice recognized the validity of the straight baseline method employed by Norway. The Court noted that though the method of following the low-water mark of the coast "in all its sinuosities . . . may be applied without difficulty to an ordinary coast, which is not too broken, . . . where a coast is deeply indented and cut into . . . or where it is bordered by an archipelago" a more practical method must be applied. 1951 I.C.J. 116, 128–29. The Court imposed certain limitations on the use of straight baselines. They "must not depart to any appreciable extent from the general direction of the coast"; the "areas lying within these lines" must be "sufficiently closely linked to the land domain to be subject to the regime of internal waters"; and account should be taken of "certain economic interests peculiar to a region, the reality and importance of which are clearly evidenced by a long usage," in determining the appropriateness of straight baselines in a particular area. Id. at 133. These concepts were incorporated in Article 4(2) and (4) of the 1958 Territorial Sea Convention and in Article 7(3) and (5) of the LOS Convention. The Court stated that the allowable length of a straight baseline is not limited by rules of international law as urged by the United Kingdom. 1951 I.C.J. 128–29. While the two conventions cited above contain no limitations on straight baselines of mainland states, the LOS Convention established a basic limit of 100 miles on the length of archipelagic baselines. Article 47(2). See Section I, infra.

Straight baselines may not be drawn to and from low-tide elevations, unless lighthouses or similar installations which are permanently above sea level have been built on them. 1958 Territorial Sea Convention, Article 4(3); LOS Convention, Article 7(4). The LOS Convention has excepted from this limitation baselines to and from such elevations which have received general international recognition. Article 7(4).

Where the presence of a delta or other natural conditions cause the coastline to be highly unstable, the appropriate points from which the straight baselines are drawn may be selected along the furthest seaward extent of the low-water line and shall remain effective until changed by the coastal state. LOS Convention, Article 7(2). See also Section C, supra.

The system of straight baselines may not be applied by a state in such a manner as to cut off the territorial sea of another state from the high seas or an exclusive economic zone. 1958 Territorial Sea Convention, Article 4(5); LOS Convention, Article 7(6). See also id., Article 47(6) (concerning archipelagic waters) and Section I, infra.

Where the establishment of a straight baseline encloses as internal waters areas which had not previously been considered as such, the coastal state must grant the right of innocent passage. LOS Convention, Article 8(2).

The United States has refrained from using straight baselines. In United States v. California, California claimed certain waters shoreward of a straight baseline running from Point Conception around the seaward side of relevant islands to Point Loma as inland waters, even though the United States government had consistently used the normal baseline method. The Court found that the decision to use straight baselines "is one that rests with the Federal Government, and not with the individual States." 381 U.S. 139, 168 (1965). But see with respect to the practice of states in establishing historic title United States v. Louisiana, 394 U.S. 11, 76–78 (1969) (the Special Master should consider a state's exercise of dominion as relevant to the existence of historic title).

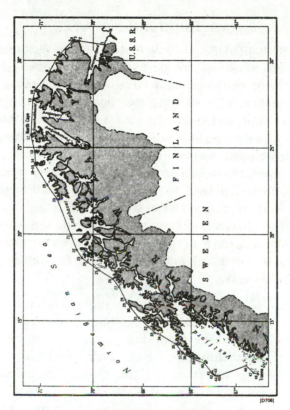

[D708]

**Illustration 2**
Straight Baselines
Drawn by Norway

## I.  ARCHIPELAGIC STATES

An archipelagic state is a state whose territory consists wholly of one or more archipelagoes.  It may include other islands (to which baselines may not be drawn), but may not possess any continental mainland territory.  An archipelagic state may "draw straight archipelagic baselines joining the outermost points of the outermost islands," and measure its territorial sea from these baselines, provided that the baselines do not exceed 100 nautical miles (with some exceptions), and that the areas thus encompassed include the main islands and have a ratio of water-area to land-area between 1 to 1 and 9 to 1.  LOS Convention, Articles 46–47.

The use of such baselines is subject to certain limitations.  The baselines shall not depart to any appreciable extent from the general configuration of the archipelago.  Such baselines shall not be drawn to and from low-tide elevations, unless lighthouses or similar installations which are permanently above sea level have been built on them or where a low-tide elevation is situated wholly or partly within the territorial sea of the nearest island.  The system of straight baselines shall not be applied in such a manner as to cut off from the high seas or the exclusive economic zone the territorial sea of another state.  If a part of the archipelagic waters lies between two parts of a

[56]

neighboring state, that state has the right to continue to exercise all rights it has traditionally exercised in such waters. Id., Article 47(3)–(6).

The United States has in the past objected to the right of archipelagic states to draw straight baselines. The United States position has been that the baselines for measuring the territorial sea and other maritime zones are to be drawn around each island. See [1978] Digest of U.S. Practice in International Law 943. In connection with the issuance of the United States proclamation of an exclusive economic zone in March 1983, the President stated that the Law of the Sea Convention "fairly balances the interests of all states . . . relating to the traditional uses of the oceans— such as navigation and overflight," and that the United States was ready to accept and act in accordance with this balance. He announced that in this respect "the United States will recognize the rights of other states in the waters off their coasts, as reflected in the Convention, so long as the rights and freedoms of the United States and others under international law are recognized by such coastal states." 23 I.L.M. 464 (1983). It appears that the United States might be willing to recognize the rights of archipelagic states under the Convention, provided they observe the provisions of that Convention relating to the right of archipelagic sea lanes passage.  LOS Convention, Article 53.

If a state possesses an archipelago away from its continental mass, it is not entitled to the special treatment accorded archipelagic states, and archipelagic baselines may not be drawn by states which do not qualify as archipelagic states.

## J.   HISTORIC INLAND WATERS, INCLUDING HISTORIC BAYS

The International Court of Justice has defined "historic waters" as internal waters "which would not have that character were it not for the existence of an historic title."  Fisheries Case (U. K. v. Norway), 1951 I.C.J. 116, 130.  Three factors are considered in determining whether a state has acquired historic title in coastal waters: (1) the state must exercise sovereign authority over the area; (2) such exercise of authority must have been exercised regularly for a considerable time; and (3) other states must acquiesce in such exercise of authority.  U.N. Secretariat, Juridical Regime of Historic Waters, Including Historic Bays, U.N. Doc. A/CN.4/143 (1962), [1962] 2 Y.B. Int'l L.Comm'n 1, 13.  See also U.N. Secretariat, Historic Bays, U.N. Doc. A/CONF.13/1 (1957), 1 UNCLOS I, Off. Rec. 1 (U.N. Pub. No. 58.V.4, Vol. I).

In Louisiana v. United States, Louisiana argued that the regulation of navigation over certain coastal waters had given rise to historic title over the waters as inland waters. The Court held that the exercise of authority necessary to establish historic title must be commensurate in scope with the nature of the title claimed, and that the regulation of innocent passage characterized the waters at most as territorial sea rather than inland waters. 394 U.S. 11, 24–26 (1969). In the same case, the United States contended that the activities of Louisiana should not be considered in determining the existence of historic title. The Court stated that even where the United States disclaims historic title, a case may arise where there are sufficient state activities to establish historic title prior to any disclaimer by the United States, but that Louisiana did not prove the existence of such activities. Id. at 76–78 (1969).

In United States v. Alaska, Alaska claimed historic title to Cook Inlet on the basis of federal and Alaskan regulation of fish and wildlife. The Supreme Court found that the enforcement of fish and wildlife regulations was insufficient in scope to establish historic title to Cook Inlet as inland waters. 422 U.S. 184, 197 (1975).

For a listing of historic bays around the world, see 4 Whiteman, Digest of International Law 233–39 (1965).

# CHAPTER IV

# BOUNDARIES OF MARITIME JURIS-DICTION BETWEEN ADJACENT AND OPPOSITE STATES

## A. TERRITORIAL SEA

Unless otherwise agreed between them, where the coasts of two states are opposite or adjacent to each other, neither state is entitled to extend its territorial sea beyond the median line every point of which is equidistant from the nearest points on the baseline from which the breadth of the territorial sea is measured. However, this rule does not apply where historic title or other special circumstances require a different delimitation. 1958 Territorial Sea Convention, Article 12; LOS Convention, Article 15.

The equidistance method had been used in several early treaties between adjacent and opposite states, primarily in situations of opposite coasts. See, e.g., 1846 United States-Great Britain Treaty, Article 1 (establishing boundary in the Juan de Fuca Straits); 1910 United States-Great Britain Boundary Treaty, Article 1 (establishing boundary in Passamaquoddy Bay). In 1953, a Committee of Experts consulted by the International Law Commission recommended the equidistance method, provided that where the presence of special circumstances led to an inequitable solution, a boundary be drawn by agreement. [1953] 2 Y.B. Int'l L.Comm'n 77, 79. Concerning methods of drawing equidistance boundaries, see Boggs, International Boundaries 176–92 (1940).

On the basis of the report of the Committee of Experts, the International Law Commission agreed quickly on applying the median line between opposite states, unless another boundary is justified by special circumstance. It encountered more difficulties with respect to the boundary line between two adjacent states. Before settling on the equidistance-special circumstances combination, the Commission explored alternatives. For instance, it considered a boundary drawn perpendicular to the general direction of the coast, a method applied in the 1909 Hague Arbitration award regarding the Norwegian-Swedish maritime boundary. The Grisbadarna Case, 1 Scott, The Hague Court Reports 121, 129 (1916). The Committee of Experts consulted by the Commission found that this rule involved the difficulty of choosing an arbitrary stretch of coast to determine "the general direction of the coast." U.N. Doc. A/3159 (1956); [1956] 2 Y.B. Int'l L. Comm'n 253, 272. The Commission also found impracticable a line drawn at right angles to the coast where the land frontier reaches the sea, which could cause the line to meet the coast at another point in the presence of a curvature of the coast.  Id.  The Commission rejected as well a boundary which represented the continuance of the land frontier boundary, finding such a proposal impracticable where the land boundary meets the coast at an acute angle.  Similarly, the Commission found that a line tracing the geographical parallel passing through the point at which the land frontier meets the coast would not be appropriate in all cases.  Id.

The equidistance principle cannot be applied if the presence of special circumstances requires another boundary in order to reach an equitable solution.  "Equidistance" and "special circumstances" are two integral components of a single rule. 1977 France-United Kingdom Continental Shelf Arbitration, 18 U.N.R.I.A.A. 3, 44–45, 18 I.L.M. 397, 421 (1979).  In its final draft on the regime of territorial waters, the International Law Commission noted as possible "special circumstances" the presence of islands or navigable channels near the baseline and an exceptional configuration of the coast.  [1956] 2 Y.B. Int'l L. Comm'n 253, 300. For an example of a special circumstance requiring the modification of an equidistant line, see the 1970 United States-Mexico Boundary Treaty establishing a 12-mile lateral boundary which did not take into account certain islands.

The existence of historic title, including historic fishing rights, "founded on the vital needs of the population and attested by very ancient and peaceful usage," has been acknowledged by the International Court of Justice as a factor which may "legitimately be taken into account in drawing a line." The Fisheries Case (U. K. v. Norway), 1951 I.C.J. 116, 142. See also the Grisbadarna Case, 1 Scott, The Hague Court Reports 121, 130–31 (1916); Continental Shelf Case (Tunisia-Libya), 1982 I.C.J. 18, 71–75.

The continental shelf and the exclusive economic zone start where the territorial sea ends; they do not overlap the territorial sea. 1958 Convention on the Continental Shelf, Article 1; LOS Convention, Articles 55 and 76.

## B. CONTINENTAL SHELF AND EXCLUSIVE ECONOMIC ZONE

### 1. *General Rule—Delimitation by Agreement*

The delimitation of the exclusive economic zone and continental shelf between adjacent or opposite states shall be determined by agreement. 1958 Convention on the Continental Shelf, Article 6; LOS Convention Articles 74 and 83. In the North Sea Continental Shelf Cases, 1969 I.C.J. 3, 47, the International Court of Justice stated that under international law:

> [T]he parties are under an obligation to enter into negotiations with a view to arriving at an agreement, and not merely to go through a formal process of negotiation as a

[*63*]

sort of prior condition for the automatic application of a certain method of delimitation in the absence of an agreement; they are under an obligation so to conduct themselves that the negotiations are meaningful, which will not be the case when either of them insists upon its own position without contemplating any modification of it.

Pending agreement, the states concerned shall make every effort to enter into provisional arrangements. LOS Convention, Articles 74 and 83. See, for example, § 202(d) of the Fishery Conservation and Management Act, 16 U.S.C. § 1822(d) (1976), which has been used by the President as authority to enter into provisional agreements concerning fishing areas where the United States 200-mile fishery conservation zone overlaps the maritime zones of other coastal states. After a series of provisional agreements, maritime boundary treaties were concluded. See 1977 United States-Cuba Maritime Boundary Treaty; 1978 United States-Mexico Maritime Boundary Treaty; 1978 United States-Venezuela Maritime Boundary Treaty. Each treaty was negotiated "on the basis of equitable principles in light of the relevant geographic circumstances." [1978] Digest of U.S. Practice in International Law 945–49; Feldman & Colson, "The Maritime Boundaries of the United States," 75 A.J.I.L. 729 (1981). See also Burmester, "The Torres Strait Treaty: Ocean

Boundary Delimitation by Agreement," 76 A.J.I.L. 321 (1982).

In a few situations, states have entered boundary agreements which provide for areas of joint resource development. See, for example, the 1974 Japan-South Korea Joint Development Zone Agreement and the 1978 Indonesia-Malaysia-Thailand Continental Shelf Boundaries Agreement.

2. *Rules to be Applied in the Absence of Agreement*

Principles to be applied to delimitation of the continental shelf and the exclusive economic zone in the absence of agreement have been a source of great controversy. Article 6 of the 1958 Convention on the Continental Shelf provided that in the absence of agreement, and unless another boundary was justified by special circumstances, the continental shelf boundary shall be the median line, where opposite states are involved, and an equidistant line where adjacent states are involved. In the North Sea Continental Shelf Cases (Federal Republic of Germany—Denmark and the Netherlands), the International Court of Justice rejected the argument made by the Netherlands and Denmark that the equidistance-special circumstances rule had become a rule of customary international law applicable to continental shelf delimitations between adjacent states. 1969 I.C.J. 3, 41. The Court noted that the distortions caused by certain conditions of coastal configurations, which produce an acceptable effect within territorial waters, are magnified in the context of a continental shelf delimitation, resulting in an inequitable boundary. Id. at 37, 49.   The Court found that there is no single obligatory method of delimitation of the continental shelf, and that "delimitation is to be effected by agreement in accordance with equitable principles, and taking account of all the relevant circumstances."   Id. at 53.   Such delimitation should "leave as much as possible to each Party all those parts of the continental shelf that constitute a natural prolongation of its land territory into and under the sea, without encroachment on the natural prolongation of the land territory of the other."   Id.   The Court considered as relevant circumstances such factors as:

    (1) the general configuration of the coasts of the parties, as well as the presence of any special or unusual features;

    (2) so far as known or readily ascertainable, the physical and geological structure, and natural resources, of the continental shelf areas involved;

    (3) the element of a reasonable degree of proportionality, which a delimitation carried out in accordance with equitable principles ought to bring about between the extent of the continental shelf areas appertaining to the

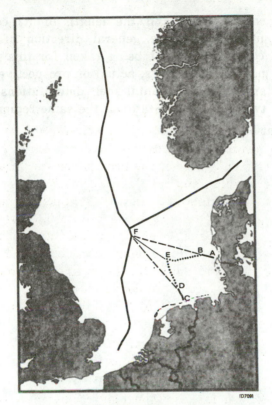

**Illustration 3**

North Sea Continental Shelf Cases

Lines A–B, C–D—Territorial Sea Boundaries

Lines B–E–F, D–E–F—Proposed
Equidistant Boundaries

Lines B–F, D–F—Boundaries Proposed by
the Federal Republic of Germany

coastal State and the length of its coast measured in the general direction of the coastline, account being taken for this purpose of the effects, actual or prospective, of any other continental shelf delimitations between adjacent States in the same region.

Id. at 54.

In 1977, a specially appointed tribunal established the continental shelf boundary between the United Kingdom and France in two geographically different areas. France-United Kingdom Continental Shelf Arbitration, 18 U.N.R.I.A.A. 3, 18 I.L.M. 397 (1979). In the eastern end of the English Channel, the British Channel Isles lay directly off the coast of France. The tribunal found that reservations made by France to Article 6 of the 1958 Convention on the Continental Shelf made the Article inapplicable to the delimitation of the Channel Isles area. However, the tribunal found that the combined equidistance-special circumstance rule of Article 6 reached the same object as that of customary international law—"the delimitation of a boundary in accordance with equitable principles." Id. at 422 (1979). The tribunal went on to consider the location of the Channel Isles, their size, population, political and economic significance to the United Kingdom, the defense and security interests of each nation, their territorial seas and fishing regimes, and the geological unity of the continental shelf in the English Channel. Taking account of these factors, the tribunal drew a primary boundary between the two countries using a median line without taking account of the Channel Isles. A second boundary was drawn at a distance of 12 miles from the coast of the Channel Isles to their north and west, granting them an enclave within the

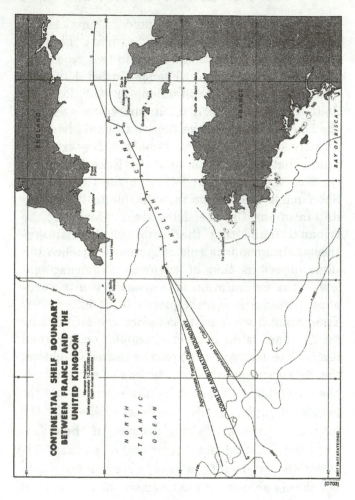

**Illustration 4**

French continental shelf; the boundary between their south and east coasts and the French coast was left to later determination.

The second area of delimitation was in the Atlantic Ocean west of the English Channel. In that area, the coast of the United Kingdom, including the Scilly Islands, extends farther west than the French mainland and the French island of Ushant. The tribunal found that Article 6 of the 1958 Convention was applicable in this situation. In the tribunal's view, the extension of the Scillies farther west from the British coast than the distance between Ushant and the French coast constituted a special circumstance which would result in an inequitable boundary if the equidistance method were applied without modification. The tribunal drew a boundary which was halfway between an equidistant line determined using Ushant and the Scillies and an equidistant line that disregarded the Scillies and was determined from Ushant and the British mainland. Id. at 455–56.

In the Tunisia-Libyan Continental Shelf Case, the International Court of Justice found that in order to achieve "an overall equitable result" it was necessary to treat the continental shelf near the coasts of the parties differently from the area further offshore. By adopting two different delimitation methods, the Court felt it could avoid the distorting effects of certain coastal configurations which might be appropriately taken into account in delimiting a boundary close to shore. 1982 I.C.J. 3, 92–94. In determining the appropriate delimitation the Court considered as relevant circumstances the configuration of the parties' coasts, the presence of islands, the land frontier of the parties, prior conduct of the parties in granting concessions in the area, the element of a reasonable degree of proportionality, and other existing or potential continental shelf delimitations between other states in the region. Considering the land frontier between the parties and their prior conduct in establishing a boundary for the granting of petroleum concessions, the Court determined that for the sector close to shore, the boundary line should be a line perpendicular to the coast. Id. at 84. Taking into account the radical change in the general direction of the Tunisian coastline in the Gulf of Gabes, the Court applied a line parallel to the general direction of the coast, giving a modified effect to an island formation off the coast (as was done in

[72]

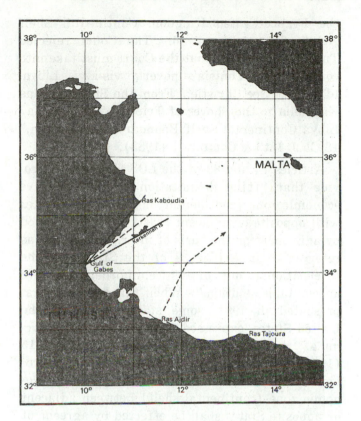

**Illustration 5**

------ Boundary Determined by the Court

the France-United Kingdom Continental Shelf Arbitration). Id. at 86. The Court rejected Tunisia's argument that the Court must take into consideration Tunisia's poverty vis-à-vis Libya. Id. at 77. See Christie, "From the Shoals of Ras Kaboudia to the Shores of Tripoli: The Tunisia/ Libya Continental Shelf Boundary Delimitation," 13 Ga.J. Int'l & Comp.L. 1 (1983).

Articles 74 and 83 of the LOS Convention provide that "[t]he delimitation of the exclusive economic zone [continental shelf] between states with opposite or adjacent coasts shall be effected by agreement on the basis of international law, as referred to in Article 38 of the Statute of the International Court of Justice, in order to achieve an equitable solution." When this test was first presented in 1981, some states, including the United States, expressed reservations to this formula. See U.N. Press Release SEA/457, at 15 (1981). An earlier draft at UNCLOS III provided that "the delimitation of the exclusive economic zone [continental shelf] between adjacent or opposite States shall be effected by agreement in accordance with equitable principles, employing, where appropriate, the median or equidistance line, and taking account of all the relevant circumstances." U.N. Doc. A/CONF.62/W.P. 10/Rev.1, 51, 57 (1979). The final text of the LOS Convention contains no direct mention of equidistance, and "equitable solution" took the place of "equitable principles." The reference to Article 38 of the Statute of the Court, which deals with the sources of international law, seems to be intended to enable the parties to rely both on the judgments of the Court and the practice of states as evidenced by the many bilateral boundary conventions concluded since 1958.

*3. United States Practice*

Under the Coastal Zone Management Act of 1972, as amended, the Assistant Administrator for Coastal Zone Management is directed to establish extensive lateral seaward boundaries between states of the United States (where not yet established by the states) for purposes of distribution of federal funds under the Coastal Energy Impact Program. 16 U.S.C. § 1456a(b)(4)(B). The Act directs the Assistant Administrator to determine the boundaries in accordance with "the applicable principles of law, including the principles of the Convention on the Territorial Sea and the Contiguous Zone, and extended on the basis of such principles." Id. The boundaries are effective only for purposes of the Act.

The committee of consultants appointed by the Assistant Administrator relied upon "the entire body of public international law relating to the delimitation of ocean boundaries," including the 1958 Conventions on the Territorial Sea and on the Continental Shelf, the North Sea Continental Shelf Cases, and the France-United Kingdom Continental Shelf Case.   Charney, "The Delimitation of Lateral Seaward Boundaries Between States in a Domestic Context," 75 A.J.I.L. 28, 33–34 (1981). The consultants determined that the boundaries should be effected in accordance with equitable principles, and that the equidistance-special circumstances rule could effect an equitable boundary.   Id. at 34 n. 29; 35 n. 31.

The five boundaries studied by the consultants were analyzed under the equidistance-special circumstances rule.   The consultants found that the presence of special circumstances in three of the areas to be delimited required the use of a line other than an equidistant line.   The special circumstances present in the Mississippi-Louisiana area were the delta and island formations.   In the New Jersey-Delaware and Delaware-Maryland areas, the concavity of the coastline was determined to be a special circumstance rendering an equidistant line inequitable.   The consultants proposed modified equidistant lines in all of these areas, based upon the France-United Kingdom Continental Shelf Case tribunal's "halving" technique.   The consultants found no special circumstances present on the New York-New Jersey and New York-Rhode Island boundary areas, and proposed an equidistant line.   Id. at 54–63.

## C.  BOUNDARY DISPUTE RESOLUTION

In several instances, states have voluntarily submitted maritime boundary disputes to an international tribunal for adjudication. See, e.g., North Sea Continental Shelf Cases (Federal Republic of Germany—Denmark and the Netherlands), 1969 I.C.J. 3; France-United Kingdom Continental Shelf Case, 18 U.N.R.I.A.A. 3, 18 I.L.M. 397 (1979); Continental Shelf Case (Tunisia—Libya), 1982 I.C.J. 3; Gulf of Maine Case (Canada—United States) submitted to the International Court of Justice, 1982 I.C.J. 3.

Articles 279–296 of the LOS Convention provide general procedures for third-party settlement of disputes arising among signatories to the Convention, but Article 298 contains special provisions for boundary disputes.  It permits a state party to the Convention to make a declaration that boundary disputes arising prior to the entry into force of the Convention shall not be subject to an obligation to submit to third-party dispute settlement.  But a dispute arising subsequent to the entry into force of the Convention shall be submitted to a conciliation commission. Although the report is not binding on the parties, the Convention requires that they negotiate an agreement on the basis of the report, and if they cannot agree, that they submit the dispute to a third-party procedure entailing a binding decision.

*

# CHAPTER V

## INTERNAL WATERS AND PORTS

### A.  INTERNAL WATERS AND PORTS

Internal waters are the waters of lakes, rivers and bays landward of the baseline of the territorial sea.  1958 Territorial Sea Convention, Article 5;  LOS Convention, Article 8.  See Chapter III with regard to determination of the baseline. A "port" is "a place where ships are in the habit of coming for the purpose of loading or unloading, embarking or disembarking."  The Mowe, [1915] P. 1, 15;  2 Lloyds Prize Cas. 70.

A coastal state has full sovereignty over its internal waters and ports, as if they were part of its land territory.  Similarly, an archipelagic state has full sovereignty over the internal waters of the archipelago (as distinguished from archipelagic waters), and there is no right of innocent passage through them.  LOS Convention, Articles 50 and 52.

### B.  FREEDOM OF ACCESS TO PORTS

The 1923 Statute on the International Régime of Maritime Ports established the principle of freedom of access to ports by foreign merchant vessels on condition of reciprocity.  Although this Statute has been ratified by fewer than thirty states, it has been accepted as reflecting a customary rule of international law.   The Statute was relied upon by an arbitral tribunal for its statement that "[a]ccording to a great principle of international law, ports of every state must be open to foreign vessels and can only be closed when the vital interests of a State so require."   Saudi Arabia v. Arabian American Oil Company (ARAMCO), Award of August 23, 1938, 27 Int'l L.Rep. 117, 212 (1963).   See also 4 Whiteman, Digest of International Law 259–61 (1965).

Numerous bilatral treaties confirm the general principle of freedom of access to ports.   For instance, Article 13(1) of the 1961 United States-Belgium Treaty of Friendship, Establishment and Navigation provides:

> Vessels of either Contracting Party shall have liberty, on equal terms with vessels of the other Party and on equal terms with vessels of any third country, to come with their cargoes to all ports, places and waters of such other Party open to foreign commerce and navigation.   Such vessels and cargoes shall in the ports, places and waters of such other Party be accorded in all respects national treatment and most-favored-nation treatment.

The parameters of the principle of freedom of access to ports have not been fully delineated through applicable multilateral or national legislation. For a list of treaties containing similar clauses, see Laws and Regulations on the Régime of the Territorial Sea, U.N. Doc. ST/LEG/SER. B/6, at 687–90 (1957). Most treaties and laws grant freedom of access on the basis of equality with national vessels and most-favored-nation vessels, but this freedom is subject to reciprocity. A United States statute, for example, permits the President to suspend commercial privileges to foreign vessels whose flag state discriminates against United States vessels. 46 U.S.C. § 142. Land-locked nations may not be denied freedom of access to ports solely because of their inability to reciprocate. 1958 Convention on the High Seas, Article 3; LOS Convention, Article 131. See also Protocol to the 1923 Statute on the International Régime of Maritime Ports, para. 4.

Foreign vessels are not allowed to engage in coastal trade or national fisheries. Access is sometimes restricted for reasons of security to ports open to foreign navigation; see, for example, U.S. Executive Order No. 1613 issued September 23, 1912, prohibiting entrance to certain strategic ports by foreign commercial and noncommercial vessels without prior authorization. 4 Whiteman, Digest of International Law 408 (1965). Article 18 of the 1923 Statute on the International Régime of Maritime Ports specifically excludes its application in time of war with regard to the rights and duties of belligerents and neutrals. Article

16 of that Statute permits "[m]easures of a general or particular character which a Contracting State is obliged to take in case of an emergency affecting the safety of the State or the vital interests of the country" which temporarily prohibit free access to ports and equality of treatment. See also the Orinoco Steamship Co. Case (United States v. Venezuela, 1903), 9 U.N.R.I.A.A. 180, 203–04 ("the right to open and close, as a sovereign on its own territory, certain harbors, ports and rivers" cannot be denied "when used . . . in defense of the very existence of the Government" against revolutionary forces). In the United States the right to safeguard harbors and ports in the event of a national security emergency is granted to the Departments of Commerce and of Transportation under Executive Order No. 11490, 50 U.S.C.A.App. § 2292.

The 1962 Nuclear Ships Convention provides in Article 8 that nothing in the Convention "shall affect any right which a Contracting State may have under international law to deny access to its waters and harbours to nuclear ships licensed by another Contracting State, even when it has formally complied with all the provisions" of the Convention.

A coastal state may condition a foreign ship's access to port upon compliance with laws and regulations governing "the conduct of the business of the port." Such laws and regulations may not be discriminatory against or among foreign vessels. 1923 Statute on the International Régime of Maritime Ports, Article 3. Such regulations may include, for instance: clearance procedures, 46 U.S.C. §§ 91–113; tonnage duties, 46 U.S.C. §§ 121–135; pollution and safety controls, 33 U.S.C. §§ 1251–1265, 46 U.S.C. § 391(a); sanitary and health regulations, 42 U.S.C. § 269, 46 U.S.C. §§ 151–163; pilotage, 46 U.S.C. §§ 211–215.

A foreign vessel whose owners or operators have violated the provisions of the Shipping Act of 1916, as amended, prohibiting rebates to shippers and other discriminating or unfair methods of competition, shall be refused entrance into United States ports. 46 U.S.C. § 813.

The 1965 Maritime Traffic Convention establishes standards and recommends practices with respect to documents that may be required to be submitted upon port entrance. The International Maritime Organization (IMO, formerly IMCO), has developed standardized shipping documents. Several conventions, such as the 1966 Load Lines Convention and the 1973 Convention for the Prevention of Pollution from Ships, provide for standard certificates relating to a vessel's loadlines, pollution-prevention standards, safety standards, and tonnage. The certificates must be accepted at ports of parties to the Convention as evidence that the foreign vessel complies with applicable requirements.

The occurrence of numerous navigational accidents involving oil tankers in the late 1970's resulted in regulations aimed at achieving safer and less polluting tanker vessels. The United States enacted laws and regulations conditioning port entrance on compliance with new safety and anti-pollution standards. For example, under Navigational Safety Regulations issued by the United States Department of Transportation in 1977, all large vessels destined for United States ports or internal waters must test certain equipment 12 hours prior to entering United States navigable waters. 33 C.F.R. § 164.25. The Port and Waterways Safety Act of 1972, as amended, imposes, among other restrictions, stricter equipment and construction requirements on large vessels, 46 U.S.C. § 391a, and it prohibits any vessel deemed "unsafe" and which has not been issued a certificate of compliance under the Act from entering into or operating in United States navigable waters. 33 U.S.C. § 1228; 46 U.S.C. § 391a(8). The Coast Guard has authority under 46 U.S.C. § 391a(10) to prescribe manning standards for foreign vessels entering United States navigable waters, which are destined for a United States port and are carrying oil or hazardous materials. Violating vessels are subject to withholding of entry clearance as well as civil and criminal penalties. See generally Meese, "When Jurisdictional Interests Collide: International, Domestic, and State

Efforts to Prevent Vessel Source Oil Pollution,"
12 Ocean Dev. & Int'l L.J. 71 (1982). In Ray v.
Atlantic Richfield Co., the Supreme Court held
that Title II of the Ports and Waterways Safety
Act of 1972, 46 U.S.C. § 391a, intended to create
uniform national standards for the design and construction of tankers, and thus preempted the high-
er standards legislated by the State of Washington. 435 U.S. 151 (1978).

See generally, with regard to the principle of
freedom of access to ports, UNCTAD Secretariat,
Report on the Treatment of Foreign Merchant
Vessels in Ports, U.N. Doc. TD/B/C.4/136
(1975) and U.N. Doc. TD/B/C.4/158 (1977);
Lowe, "The Right of Entry into Maritime Ports
in International Law," 14 San Diego L.Rev. 597
(1977).

## C. JURISDICTION OVER FOREIGN VESSELS WHILE IN PORT

A foreign merchant ship which voluntarily enters the ports or internal waters of a coastal
state subjects itself fully to the administrative,
civil and criminal jurisdiction of that state, unless otherwise agreed by treaty between the
coastal state and the flag state. Wildenhus' Case,
120 U.S. 1, 11 (1887). In particular, every foreign ship, including warships, must comply in
port or internal waters with the laws and regulations of the coastal state relating to navigation,
safety, health and port administration.

The coastal state "may out of considerations of public policy choose to forego the exertion of its jurisdiction or to exert the same only in a limited way, but this is a matter resting solely in its discretion."   Cunard S.S. Co. v. Mellon, 262 U.S. 100, 124 (1922).   In order to facilitate the free flow of international trade, coastal states generally do not exert their jurisdiction, and they leave a ship's internal matters which do not involve the "peace or dignity" of the coastal state or the "tranquillity of the port" to the authorities of the nation under whose flag the vessel flies. Wildenhus' Case, 120 U.S. 1, 12 (1887).   A murder of one crewman by another committed in a port on board a foreign vessel is, however, a matter which disturbs the tranquillity of the port and is subject to local jurisdiction.   Id. at 18.

Numerous bilateral agreements reflect this principle.   For instance, the 1951 United States-United Kingdom Consular Convention provides in Article 22(2):

> [T]he administrative and police authorities of the territory should not, except at the request or with the consent of the consular officer,
>
> (a) concern themselves with any matter taking place on board the vessel unless for the preservation of peace and order or in the interests of public health or safety, or

(b) institute prosecutions in respect of crimes or offenses committed on board the vessel unless they are of a serious character or involve the tranquillity of the port or unless they are committed by or against persons other than the crew.

See also 22 U.S.C. §§ 256–258 setting forth procedures to be followed by a foreign consul in the arrest of foreign seamen while in United States ports.

Where it chooses, the coastal state may extend its jurisdiction to matters relating to the internal affairs of the ships and to acts which do not disturb the peace of the port. For example, a provision of the Seamen's Act of 1915, making it unlawful to pay seamen's wages in advance, specifically applies to foreign vessels while in United States waters. 46 U.S.C. § 599(e). In Cunard S.S. Co. v. Mellon, the Supreme Court found a congressional intent that the prohibition statutes were to be applied everywhere within the jurisdiction of the United States, including foreign vessels in United States ports. 262 U.S. 100 (1922).

Where there is no express statutory extension of jurisdiction over the internal affairs of a ship, it is the practice of United States courts not to apply United States law affecting internal management to foreign flag vessels in United States ports. See, for example, Benz v. Compania Naviera Hidalgo, S.A., 353 U.S. 138 (1957) (Labor Management Relations Act not applicable to the internal labor relations of a foreign ship and its foreign crew while in a United States port absent a clear statement of congressional intent to that effect); McCulloch v. Sociedad Nacional de Marineros de Honduras, 372 U.S. 10 (1962) (National Labor Relations Act not intended to be applied to foreign vessels employing foreign seamen). See also May, "The Status of Federal Maritime Commission Shipping Regulation under Principles of International Law," 54 Georgetown L.J. 794 (1966).

In extending United States civil jurisdiction under the Jones Act, 46 U.S.C. § 688, which provides to seamen injured in the course of employment an action for damages, United States courts have developed a contacts test in determining whether to apply the Act to foreign seamen injured on foreign vessels. See Chapter II, Section B.9, supra. The fact that an injury occurs while a foreign vessel is in a United States port is insufficient of itself to confer jurisdiction on United States courts. See, for instance, Rodriguez v. Orion Schiffahrts-Gesellschaft Reith & Co., 348 F.Supp. 777 (S.D.N.Y.1972); Katelouzos v. The S.S. Othem, 184 F.Supp. 526 (E.D.Va.1960).

Where a person, before boarding a ship, has committed a crime in the territory of a foreign state, that person is not entitled to asylum aboard the ship after it has entered a port or internal waters of a third state. In the Eisler case, Poland protested the arrest of Eisler, a Polish national, by British authorities on board a Polish vessel while in a British port. The United States had requested the arrest and extradition for a crime committed in the United States. In its reply to Poland, the British government, after citing numerous instances of arrest by local authorities of persons seeking refuge on foreign vessels, concluded:

> The absence of any right to grant asylum on board merchant ships, and consequently the right of the coastal authority to arrest a person on board, either for an offense committed by him on shore or in virtue of a request for his extradition under an extradition treaty with another country in which he has committed an offence, springs from the principle of international law, universally recognised by the authorities, that a merchant ship in the ports or roadsteads of another country falls under the jurisdiction of the coastal state.

The British government further stated that the right of the coastal state to act did not depend on prior request for assistance by the vessel's captain or the flag state's consular officer, since the crime did not occur in port or on the vessel.   9

Whiteman, Digest of International Law 135–36 (1968).

Where a foreign vessel seeks refuge in the ports or internal waters of a coastal state due to distress or force majeure, the principles of coastal state jurisdiction discussed above do not apply, and the foreign ship is immune from coastal state jurisdiction. For example, such vessels are not subject to coastal state customs laws. Kate A. Hoff Claim (United States v. Mexico), 4 U.N.R.I. A.A. 444 (1929).

For a discussion of coastal state jurisdiction over foreign warships and government noncommercial vessels, see Chapter II, Section B.8., supra.

## D.  JURISDICTION OF FLAG STATE OVER VESSELS IN FOREIGN PORTS OR INTERNAL WATERS

Where the coastal state does not assert jurisdiction over an offense on the ground that it has disturbed the peace of the port, "it is the duty of the courts of the flag state to apply to offenses committed by its citizens on vessels flying its flag, its own statutes." United States v. Flores, 289 U.S. 137, 158–59 (1933). In that case, a United States citizen murdered another United States citizen while aboard a United States merchant vessel docked at a river port 250 miles inland in the Belgian Congo. The Belgian authorities did not take any steps to punish the crime, and the Supreme Court upheld United States jurisdiction on the principle that a merchant vessel is deemed "to be part of the territory" of the United States.

In United States v. Reagan, a crew member of United States nationality was accused of killing another crew member of United States nationality on a United States vessel in a German harbor. The defendant had been taken into custody by German authorities and was committed to a German mental institution. He was subsequently released. The court held that these "preliminary proceedings" did not constitute an assertion of jurisdiction sufficient "to oust the jurisdiction of the flag sovereign." 453 F.2d 165, 171 (6th Cir. 1971).

## E. ENLARGED PORT STATE JURISDICTION

The LOS Convention authorizes a "port state" to undertake investigations and institute proceedings in respect of any discharge from a ship "voluntarily within a port or at an offshore terminal" in violation of applicable international rules and standards, that has occurred not only "within the territorial sea or the exclusive economic zone of that state," but also "outside the internal waters, territorial sea, or exclusive economic zone of the State." Articles 218(1) and 220(1). If the discharge has occurred in the coastal waters of another state, proceedings may be instituted in the port state only on request of that coastal state, or the flag state, or of a state damaged or threatened by the discharge. If the state that has requested the initiation of the proceedings in the port state so asks, the proceedings may be transferred to it. Even if the proceedings were not instituted at the request of the flag state, it may request suspension and initiate its own proceedings. However, a port state that has instituted the original proceedings need not suspend them if they relate to a case of major damage to the port state, or if the flag state in question "has repeatedly disregarded its obligations to enforce effectively the applicable international rules and standards in respect of violations committed by its vessels." Id., Articles 218(2)–(4) and 228. To mitigate the high cost of holding violating vessels in port, the ship must be permitted to proceed upon posting of a bond or other appropriate financial security. Id., Article 220(7). See also Articles 228 and 292.

In recent years, numerous other international measures have been adopted or proposed which aim at encouraging port states to exercise limited jurisdiction over the safety and social standards of foreign merchant vessels entering their ports. In 1975, the International Maritime Organization (IMO, formerly IMCO) adopted the "Procedures for the Control of Ships" setting forth guidelines to port states as to their powers of inspection and detention of foreign merchant vessels under the 1960 Safety of Life at Sea Convention and the 1966 Load Lines Convention. See also the 1982 Memorandum of Understanding on Port State Control between fourteen European countries. The Minimum Standards in Merchant Ships Convention, adopted by the International Labor Conference in 1976, authorizes contracting port states to inspect foreign merchant vessels, regardless of whether the flag state has ratified the Convention, and to take remedial measures if the vessel does not meet labor conditions specified in the Convention.

## F.  DEEPWATER PORTS

For a discussion of a coastal state's jurisdiction over deepwater ports constructed in its territorial sea or exclusive economic zone, see Chapter VII, Section I, infra.

# CHAPTER VI

# THE TERRITORIAL SEA

## A. COASTAL STATE SOVEREIGNTY OVER THE TERRITORIAL SEA

Subject to the right of innocent passage through the territorial sea and to special passage rights through straits and archipelagic waters, the coastal state has the same sovereignty over its territorial sea and over the air space, seabed and subsoil thereof, as it has with respect to its land territory. 1958 Territorial Sea Convention, Articles 1–2; LOS Convention, Article 2.

Prior to the Second World War, the sovereignty of the coastal state over its territorial sea was contested, as some courts (especially French ones) and writers had characterized the territorial sea as part of the high seas subject to special rights for the coastal states. See 1 Oppenheim, International Law 487 (Lauterpacht 8th ed. 1955). The sovereignty of a coastal state over its territorial sea has since been accepted as customary international law, and is recognized by the 1958 Territorial Sea Convention, Articles 1 and 2, and the LOS Convention, Article 2.

## B.  BREADTH OF THE TERRITORIAL SEA

Every state has the right to establish the breadth of its territorial sea up to a limit not exceeding 12 nautical miles, measured from the baseline as determined in accordance with the principles discussed in Chapter III. When states first began exercising their sovereign rights in the territorial sea, most established a 3-mile belt of jurisdiction, based upon the range of a cannon. However, in the twentieth century, many states extended the breadth of their territorial sea, first to six miles and later to twelve miles, though in some instances claims were made of up to 200 miles. Several major maritime nations, including the United States, strongly opposed extended claims of territorial sea jurisdiction as an intrusion upon the freedoms of the high seas. See United States Notes of July 2, 1948 to the Governments of Peru, Chile, and Argentina in 4 Whiteman, Digest of International Law 793, 796, 798 (1965).

The International Law Commission reported in 1956 that there was no uniform practice regarding the breadth of the territorial sea, but stated that "international law does not permit that limit to be extended beyond 12 miles." [1956] 2 Y.B. Int'l L. Comm'n 253, 265–66. After much debate between proponents of a 3-mile limit to the territorial sea and proponents of an extended territorial sea, the 1958 Conference on the Law of the Sea failed to establish a uniform limit to the breadth of the territorial sea. The 1960 Conference also failed to agree on the limit. 4 Whiteman, Digest of International Law 91–137 (1965).

An increasing number of states extended their claims of a territorial sea in the 1960's and 1970's from three miles up to as much as 200 miles. See, for instance, Ecuador, Decree of 1966 establishing a 200-mile territorial sea, National Legislation and Treaties Relating to the Law of the Sea, U.N. Doc. ST/LEG/SER.B/15, at 78–79 (1970). The need for a uniform limit to the breadth of the territorial sea was again the subject of much debate in the Third United Nations Conference on the Law of the Sea. The Conference finally accepted a limit of twelve nautical miles. LOS Convention, Article 3.

The United States continues to adhere to a 3-mile territorial sea. For a discussion of the history of the establishment by the United States of a 3-mile territorial sea, see United States v. California, 332 U.S. 19, 32–34 (1947). For a list of limits of the claims of other states to their territorial seas, see U.S. Department of State, National Claims to Maritime Jurisdiction (Limits in the Seas, No. 36, 3d rev. 1975).

## C.  THE RIGHT OF INNOCENT PASSAGE

An exception to the sovereignty of a coastal state over its territorial sea is the right of ships of all states to innocent passage through the territorial sea of any coastal state.  1958 Territorial Sea Convention, Article 14; LOS Convention, Article 17.  Passage means navigation through the territorial sea for the purpose of either traversing that sea without entering internal waters, or proceeding to or from internal waters.  Passage must be continuous and expeditious, but a ship may stop and anchor if this is incidental to ordinary navigation, is rendered necessary by force majeure or is required in order to assist persons, ships or aircraft in danger or distress. 1958 Territorial Sea Convention, Article 14(3); LOS Convention, Article 18(2).

Passage is innocent so long as it is not prejudicial to the peace, good order or security of the coastal state.  1958 Territorial Sea Convention, Article 14(4);  LOS Convention, Article 19(1). Passage is not innocent if a foreign ship engages in any of the following activities while in the territorial sea of the coastal state and without the consent of the coastal state:

> (a) any threat or use of force against the sovereignty, territorial integrity or political independence of the coastal state, or in any other manner in violation of the principles

of international law embodied in the Charter of the United Nations;

(b) any exercise or practice with weapons of any kind;

(c) any act aimed at collecting information to the prejudice of the defense or security of the coastal state;

(d) any act of propaganda aimed at affecting the defense or security of the coastal state;

(e) the launching, landing or taking on board of any aircraft;

(f) the launching, landing or taking on board of any military device;

(g) the loading or unloading of any commodity, currency or person contrary to the customs, fiscal, immigration or sanitary laws and regulations of the coastal state;

(h) any act of wilful and serious pollution in contravention of international law;

(i) any fishing activities;

(j) the carrying out of research or survey activities;

(k) any act aimed at interfering with any systems of communication or any other facilities or installations of the coastal state; or

[98]

(*l*) any other activity not having a direct bearing on passage.

LOS Convention, Article 19(2).

The coastal state may not hamper the innocent passage of foreign ships through its territorial sea except in accordance with international law. 1958 Territorial Sea Convention, Article 15(1); LOS Convention, Article 24(1). However, the coastal state has the unilateral right to verify the innocent character of passage, and it may take the necessary steps in its territorial sea to prevent passage which it determines to be not innocent. In the case of ships proceeding to internal waters or ports, the coastal state has the right to prevent any breach of the conditions to which admission of those ships is subject. 1958 Territorial Sea Convention, Article 16(2); LOS Convention, Article 25(2). The coastal state may also, without discrimination, suspend temporarily in specified areas of its territorial sea the innocent passage of ships if such suspension is essential for the protection of its security, including weapons exercises. Suspension may take effect only after due publication. 1958 Territorial Sea Convention, Article 16(3); LOS Convention, Article 25(3). Authorization to suspend innocent passage in the United States territorial sea during a national emergency is given to the President in 50 U.S.C. § 191. For instances in which innocent passage has been suspended, see 4 Whiteman, Digest of International Law 379–86 (1965).

The coastal state may adopt laws and regulations relating to innocent passage through the territorial sea only with regard to certain specified subjects, namely: the safety of navigation and the regulation of maritime traffic; the protection of navigational aids and facilities and other facilities and installations; the protection of cables and pipelines; the conservation of living resources; the preservation of the environment of the coastal state and the prevention, reduction and control of pollution thereof; marine scientific research; and the enforcement of fishing, customs, fiscal, immigration and sanitary regulations. LOS Convention, Article 21(1). Foreign ships must comply with these regulations. Id., Article 21(4). Such laws and regulations may not apply to the design, construction, manning or equipment of foreign ships unless such laws and regulations are in implementation of generally accepted international rules and standards. Id., Article 21(2).

The coastal state may establish sea lanes and traffic separation schemes for passage through its territorial sea, where they are necessary to ensure the safety of navigation. The coastal state is required to take into account: the recommendations of the competent international organization (primarily the International Maritime Organization (IMO, formerly IMCO)); any channels customarily used for international navigation; the special characteristics of particular ships and channels; and the density of traffic. LOS Convention, Article 22. For the international regulations concerning the routing of ships approved by the International Maritime Organization in 1973, see IMCO Doc. Res.A. 284 (VIII), 4 Churchill & Nordquist, New Directions in the Law of the Sea 235-43 (1975), and for their application by the United States, see 33 C.F.R. §§ 80-82. Foreign ships must comply with these sea lanes and traffic schemes. LOS Convention, Article 22(1).

A coastal state should not exercise criminal jurisdiction on board a foreign ship passing through the territorial sea for the purpose of arresting a person on board the ship or of conducting any investigation, in connection with any crime committed on board the ship during its passage through the territorial sea, unless:

> (a) the consequences of the crime extend to the coastal state;
>
> (b) the crime is of a kind to disturb the peace of the country or the good order of the territorial sea;
>
> (c) the assistance of the local authorities has been requested by the master of the ship or by a diplomatic agent or consular officer of the flag state; or

> (d)  such measures are necessary for the suppression of illicit traffic in narcotic drugs.

1958 Territorial Sea Convention, Article 19(1); LOS Convention, Article 27(1). See, with respect to measures enacted to prevent drug trafficking, 21 U.S.C. § 955.

The coastal state may not take any steps on board a foreign ship passing through the territorial sea to arrest any person or to conduct any investigation in connection with any crime committed before the ship entered the territorial sea, if the ship, proceeding from a foreign port, is only passing through the territorial sea without entering internal waters, unless otherwise permitted under international law (see Chapter V, Section E). 1958 Territorial Sea Convention, Article 19(5); LOS Convention, Article 27(5).

Similarly, the coastal state should not exercise its civil jurisdiction over foreign ships passing through the territorial sea in relation to a person on board the ship. The coastal state may not levy execution against or arrest the ship for the purpose of any civil proceedings, save only in respect of obligations or liabilities assumed or incurred by the ship itself in the course or for the purpose of its voyage through the waters of the coastal state. However, a coastal state may levy execution against or arrest for civil proceedings a foreign ship lying in the territorial sea or passing through the territorial sea after leaving internal waters. 1958 Territorial Sea Convention, Article 20; LOS Convention, Article 28.

In 1975, a United States merchant vessel was seized by Cambodian naval forces while in passage through waters claimed by Cambodia as its territorial sea. The United States protested the seizure as occurring on the high seas and, in the alternative, as a violation of the principle of innocent passage. Military force was used to secure the vessel's release. See [1975] Digest of U.S. Practice in International Law 423; Note, "The Mayaguez: The Right of Innocent Passage and the Legality of Reprisal," 13 San Diego L. Rev. 765 (1976).

Several proposals for requiring previous notification or even authorization for the innocent passage of a warship through the territorial sea were discussed at the First and Third Conferences on the Law of the Sea, but none of the provisions were adopted. See 4 Whiteman, Digest of International Law 404–17 (1965); U.N. Doc. A/CONF.62/C.2/L.16, Article 15 (1974); 3 UNCLOS III, Official Records 194 (1974); U.N. Doc. A/CONF.26/C.2/WP.1, at 29 (1974). A number of states entered reservations imposing such requirements when ratifying the 1958 Territorial Sea Convention. 4 Whiteman, Digest of International Law 404–17 (1965). The United States adheres to the position that no prior notification is required for warships in innocent passage. [1976] Digest of U.S. Practice in International Law 343–44. For legislation requiring prior notification, see, e.g., East German Regulations, National Legislation and Treaties Relating to the Law of the Sea, U.N. Doc. ST/LEG/ SER.B/18, at 54 (1976). See generally Comment, "The Innocent Passage of Warships in Foreign Territorial Seas: A Threatened Freedom," 15 San Diego L.Rev. 573 (1978).

A warship is defined as "a ship belonging to the armed forces of a State bearing the external marks distinguishing such ships of its nationality, under the command of an officer duly commissioned by the government of the State and whose name appears in the appropriate service list or its equivalent, and manned by a crew which is under regular armed forces discipline." LOS Convention, Article 29. See also 1958 Convention on the High Seas, Article 8(2).

A warship which does not comply with the applicable laws and regulations of the coastal state and disregards any request for compliance may be required to leave the territorial sea immediately by the coastal state. 1958 Territorial Sea Convention, Article 23; LOS Convention, Article 30. See, also Netherlands Decree of October 30, 1909, Laws and Regulations on the Régime of the Territorial Sea, U.N. Doc. ST/LEG/SER.B/6, at 385, 388 (1957).

Submarines and other underwater vehicles passing through the territorial sea must navigate on the surface and show their flag. 1958 Territorial Sea Convention, Article 14(6); LOS Convention, Article 20.

Due to the high risk of pollution and the safety risks posed by large tankers, nuclear-powered ships and ships carrying nuclear or other inherently dangerous or noxious substances, a coastal state may require such ships to confine their passage to identified sea lanes. LOS Convention, Article 22(2). These ships are also obligated to observe special precautionary measures prescribed for them by international agreements. Id., Article 23.

The sovereignty of the coastal state in the air space above its territorial sea is not subject to any right of innocent passage except when so provided by international agreement. In fact, most coastal states have granted rights to overfly their territorial sea as part of their agreement to overflight of their territory generally. 1944 Chicago Convention on International Civil Aviation, Articles 2 and 5; 1944 International Air Services Transit Agreement, Article 1. Military and other state aircraft are not covered by these agreements and enjoy overflight or landing rights only by special agreement. See generally Lowenfeld, Aviation Law: Cases and Materials, Chapter 2 (1981).

[*105*]

## D.  TRANSIT PASSAGE

In 1949, the International Court of Justice confirmed that under customary international law, ships of all nations have the right to navigate "through straits used for international navigation between two parts of the high seas without the previous authorization of a coastal State," including warships in time of peace, "provided that such passage is innocent."  Corfu Channel Case (United Kingdom v. Albania), 1949 I.C.J. 4, 28.

The 1958 Territorial Sea Convention established the right of innocent passage "through straits which are used for international navigation between one part of the high seas and another part of the high seas or the territorial sea of a foreign State."  Though this right of transit passage was incorporated into the regime of innocent passage, it differed from it in that the states bordering the strait could in no event suspend the right of transit passage.  Id., Article 16(4).

The LOS Convention establishes a regime governing transit passage through straits which is separate from the regime governing innocent passage through territorial seas.  LOS Convention, Articles 34–45.  The establishment of a new regime governing transit passage resulted from the demands of major maritime states which were unwilling to accept the extension of the breadth of the territorial sea to twelve miles without a guarantee of unimpeded passage through the more than 100 straits affected by that extension. For a statement of the United States position, see [1976] Digest of U.S. Practice in International Law 341–42.

Transit passage means navigation or overflight for the purpose of continuous and expeditious transit of a strait between two areas of the high seas or between two exclusive economic zones. LOS Convention, Article 38(2). Ships and aircraft exercising the right of transit passage must proceed without delay and refrain from any activities other than those incidental to their normal modes of passage, unless rendered necessary by force majeure or by distress. Id., Article 39. Unlike innocent passage, transit passage extends to aircraft, and submarines are permitted to navigate in their "normal mode," i.e., underwater.

The fields in which a state bordering a strait may regulate transit passage are more limited than those subject to the jurisdiction of coastal states to regulate innocent passage. A state bordering on a strait may put into effect international standards and regulations regarding pollution control; it may regulate fishing activities; and it may enact customs, fiscal, immigration and sanitary regulations. Id., Article 42. These laws and regulations may not discriminate against foreign ships or in any way act to impede transit passage. Id. Foreign ships may not conduct any research or survey activities without the prior authorization of the states bordering the strait. Id., Article 40. The flag state is responsible for any loss or damage resulting from violations by a ship or aircraft enjoying sovereign immunity of laws and regulations enacted by bordering states to regulate transit passage. Id., Article 42(5).

The rights accorded states bordering straits with regard to transit passage, apart from regulatory powers, are also more limited than those granted coastal states relating to innocent passage. States bordering straits may not hamper transit passage and do not have the right to suspend unilaterally transit passage. Id., Article 44. While in the territorial sea a coastal state may establish sea lanes and traffic separation schemes taking into account the recommendations of the competent international organization (primarily the International Maritime Organization, IMO, formerly IMCO), in international straits the designation of such lanes or schemes requires concurrent action by the strait state (or states) and the competent international organization. Id., Article 41(3)–(4).

Under the LOS Convention, a right of transit passage does not exist where a strait is broad enough to allow navigation through a high seas route in its middle or such a route through an exclusive economic zone of similar convenience with respect to navigational and hydrographic characteristics. Id., Article 36. Where a strait is formed by an island of a state bordering the strait and its mainland, transit passage shall not apply if there exists an equally convenient route through the high seas or an exclusive economic zone seaward of the island. Id., Article 38.

These rules regarding alternative routes seem to overrule the Corfu Channel Case between the United Kingdom and Albania, where the International Court of Justice held that the Corfu Channel between the mainland and the island of Corfu, though not a "necessary" route between two parts of the high seas, was a "useful route for international maritime traffic" and belonged to the "class of international highways through which passage cannot be prohibited by a coastal state in time of peace." 1949 I.C.J. 4, 28–29.

Where the strait is between an area of the high seas or an exclusive economic zone and the territorial sea of a coastal state, there is no right of transit passage; however, innocent passage cannot be suspended. 1958 Territorial Sea Convention, Article 16(4); LOS Convention, Article 45. For a discussion of the legal regime governing straits between the high seas and inland seas bordered by more than one state, see El-Baradei, "The Egyptian-Israeli Peace Treaty and Access to the Gulf of Aqaba: A New Legal Regime," 76 A.J.I.L. 532 (1982).

The LOS Convention does not affect the legal regime of straits in which passage is regulated by special international conventions of long standing, such as the 1936 Montreux Straits Convention concerning the regime of the straits leading to the Black Sea.

For a discussion of the new legal regime governing transit passage, see Moore, "The Regime of Straits and the Third United Nations Conference on the Law of the Sea," 74 A.J.I.L. 77 (1980).

## E.  ARCHIPELAGIC SEA LANES PASSAGE

The LOS Convention establishes a new regime governing archipelagic waters, under which all ships enjoy the right of archipelagic sea lanes passage.  Article 53.  There are parallel rights for aircraft overflight along designated air routes.  Id.  Archipelagic sea lanes passage means navigation in the normal mode solely for the purpose of continuous and expeditious transit between two areas of the high seas or between two areas of exclusive economic zones.  Id., Article 53(3).  An archipelagic state may designate sea lanes or traffic schemes which conform to generally accepted international regulations, and any proposals for such sea lanes or traffic separation schemes must be submitted to the competent international organization (usually the International Maritime Organization) for adoption.  Id., Article 53(8)–(9).  If an archipelagic state does not designate sea lanes, the right of archipelagic sea lanes passage may be exercised through the routes normally used for international navigation. Id., Article 53(12).

In archipelagic waters other than the designated sea lanes, ships of all states enjoy the right of innocent passage, except in inland waters delimited by straight lines drawn across mouths of rivers, bays and entrances to ports. Id., Articles 50, 52 and 54.

## F. UNITED STATES TERRITORIAL SEA AND THE RIGHTS OF THE STATES

In 1947, the United States Supreme Court held that the 3-mile belt of territorial sea was "in the domain of the Nation" and that the United States was "possessed of paramount rights in, and full dominion and power over, the lands, minerals and other things" underlying the sea to the extent of three nautical miles measured from the low-water mark on the coast or from the outer limit of internal waters and that the coastal states had "no title thereto or property interest therein." United States v. California, 332 U.S. 19 and 804, 805 (Decree) (1947). See also United States v. Louisiana, 339 U.S. 699, 705 (1950); United States v. Texas, 339 U.S. 707 (1950). The Submerged Lands Act of 1953 ceded to the coastal states all the property rights of the United States in submerged lands within the 3-mile belt (and up to nine miles in the Gulf of Mexico if a state should establish a historic title to such broader area). It vested in the states "the right and power to manage, administer, lease, develop and use" the submerged land and natural resources of the ceded area, "all in accordance with applicable State law." The United States retained, however, "powers of regulation and control of said lands and navigable waters for the constitutional purposes of commerce, navigation, national defense, and international affairs." 43 U.S.C. §§ 1301–1315.

In the absence of conflicting federal legislation, the conservation and management of fisheries in the territorial sea is within the police power of the individual states. Corsa v. Tawe, 149 F.Supp. 771 (D.C.Md.1957), affirmed 355 U.S. 37 (1957). Federal laws governing the licensing of vessels have been interpreted to preempt state laws which prohibit federally licensed vessels from fishing within a state's territorial waters. Such preemption does not extend to matters other than the right to fish, such as conservation. Douglas v. Seacoast Products, Inc., 431 U.S. 265 (1977). The federal government offers assistance to the states in the development of fishery conservation and management plans in the territorial sea under the Coastal Zone Management Act of 1972, as amended, 16 U.S.C. §§ 1451 et seq.

The states have long exercised their civil and criminal jurisdiction over activities in the territorial sea. See, for instance, La.Stat.Ann.

Rev.Stat. 34:3101 et seq. (regulation of offshore terminal facilities); Official Code Ga.Ann. § 50–7–30 (promotion of marine research and industrial activities); People v. Stralla, 14 Cal.2d 617, 96 P.2d 941 (1939) (operation of a gambling ship in Santa Monica Bay subject to the California Penal Code).

## G.  CONTIGUOUS ZONE

In a zone contiguous to its territorial sea, the coastal state may exercise the control necessary to prevent infringement of its customs, fiscal, immigration or sanitary laws and regulations within its territory or territorial sea.  1958 Territorial Sea Convention, Article 24(1); LOS Convention, Article 33(1).  The contiguous zone may not extend beyond 24 nautical miles from the baseline from which the breadth of the territorial sea is measured.  LOS Convention, Article 33(2).

A United States customs officer may board any vessel within United States "customs waters" to examine its manifest and inspect and search the vessel, whether or not such vessel is bound for the United States.  19 U.S.C. § 1581.  If a violation of United States law has occurred, such vessel is subject to arrest and seizure.  Id.  "Customs waters" are defined as "the waters within four leagues of the coast of the United States" or, where a foreign vessel is subject to a treaty or other arrangement between a foreign government and the United States enabling or permitting the authorities of the United States to board such vessel, customs waters shall be the waters designated by such treaty.  19 U.S.C. § 1401(j). Under Article 2 of the 1924 United States–United Kingdom Anti-Smuggling Convention, and similar treaties with other countries, the right to board a foreign vessel may be exercised up to a distance from the coast that can be traversed by that vessel in one hour.  1 Hackworth, Digest of International Law 678–79 (1940).

The Anti-Smuggling Act of 1935, 19 U.S.C. § 1701, authorized the President to declare a "customs-enforcement area" which may extend 62 miles outward from the coast and laterally up to 100 miles in each direction.  Only five such zones were established; they were discontinued in 1946. [1948–49] U.S. Naval War College, International Legal Documents 176–80.

The United States Supreme Court upheld the right of a coastal state to exercise jurisdiction beyond the limits of its territory to prevent violation of its laws in Church v. Hubbart, 6 U.S. (2 Cranch) 186 (1809).  For a history of United States enforcement in its contiguous zone, see Jessup, The Law of Territorial Waters and Maritime Jurisdiction 241–76 (1927).  See generally Lowe, "The Development of the Contiguous Zone," 52 Brit. Y.B. Int'l L. 109 (1981).

# CHAPTER VII

# EXCLUSIVE ECONOMIC ZONE

## A. FROM FISHERY ZONES TO AN EXCLUSIVE ECONOMIC ZONE

The establishment of the exclusive economic zone (EEZ) is a recent development in international law. Until the middle of this century, all waters beyond the territorial sea and the contiguous zone were viewed as the high seas over which no state had jurisdiction. 2 Hackworth, Digest of International Law 651 (1941); 1958 Convention on the High Seas, Article 1.

The pressure for increasing the jurisdiction of coastal states over waters adjacent to the territorial sea is closely related to the growing demand for better conservation and management of coastal fisheries. Increased exploitation of fisheries in waters contiguous to the coast led several coastal states to enter bilateral and multilateral agreements to conserve and manage fisheries in contiguous zones since the beginning of the nineteenth century. See, for example, the 1818 United States-Great Britain Fisheries Convention, the 1839 France-Great Britain Fisheries Convention, the 1882 North Sea Fisheries Convention, and the 1911 Fur Seal Convention. See Riesenfeld, Protection of Coastal Fisheries Under International Law (1942).

In 1945, President Truman simultaneously issued proclamations concerning the continental shelf and coastal fisheries in certain areas of the high seas. The first proclamation asserted the right of the United States to claim jurisdiction over the natural resources of the subsoil and seabed of the continental shelf adjacent to the United States (see Chapter VIII). The fisheries proclamation asserted United States authority to establish fishery conservation zones in the high seas adjacent to its coasts on the basis that existing agreements did not adequately protect such fisheries. The United States claimed sole fishery conservation and management authority in those areas where its nationals had historically fished exclusively, and provided for joint fishery conservation and management arrangements in those areas where the nationals of other states had fished along with United States nationals. 10 Fed. Reg. 12304 (1945); 13 Dep't State Bull. 486 (1945). The United States did not, in fact, ever establish conservation zones under the authority of the proclamation.

The two proclamations prompted a number of South American states to establish zones of up to 200 miles in which they claimed complete sovereignty over the seabed, its subsoil, and superjacent waters "in order to reserve, protect, preserve and

[*116*]

exploit the natural resources of whatever nature found on, within and below the said seas." 1947 Presidential Declaration of Chile, 4 Whiteman, Digest of International Law 794–96 (1965). See also 1947 Presidential Decree No. 781 of Peru, id. at 797–98; 1951 Ecuadorean Congressional Decree, id. at 799–800. The United States objected to these and similar decrees on the bases that the decrees asserted complete national sovereignty over the zones and that they failed to accord recognition to the rights and interests of other states. Id. at 796–97, 798–99, 800–01. In 1952, Chile, Peru and Ecuador signed the Declaration of Santiago on the Maritime Zone, which proclaimed that each country possessed "sole sovereignty and jurisdiction over the area of sea adjacent to the coast of its own country and extending not less than 200 nautical miles." Id. at 1089–90. See generally Hollick, "Origins of the 200-Mile Offshore Zones," 71 A.J.I.L. 404 (1977).

The 1958 Fishing on the High Seas Convention (to which the United States and 33 other states are parties) embodies the principle of special rights of coastal states in the conservation, management and exploitation of fisheries in areas contiguous to its coast. However, the Convention does not grant coastal states exclusive rights in the conservation, management and exploitation of these fisheries, and does not apply to other resources in those areas. Article 6 provides that

[*117*]

a coastal state is entitled to take part in any fishery conservation measures in high seas adjacent to its territorial waters, even if its nationals do not fish there.  Other states whose nationals fish in that area must, at the request of the coastal state, enter negotiations with that state.  If such negotiations fail, the coastal state may unilaterally enact and enforce conservation measures that are urgently needed.  Such measures must be based on scientific findings and may not be discriminatory.  Id., Article 7.  In addition, any conservation measures must be designed to render possible "the optimum sustainable yield from those resources so as to secure a maximum supply of food and other marine products."  Id., Article 2.

After the 1960 Law of the Sea Conference failed, by one vote, to adopt a compromise solution which would have extended coastal states' exclusive fishing jurisdiction to twelve miles (see 4 Whiteman, Digest of International Law 122–37 (1965)), many states extended their exclusive fishery jurisdiction to twelve miles by national legislation.  See, for example, the Exclusive Fisheries Zone Act of 1966, 16 U.S.C. §§ 1091–1094 (establishment of a 12-mile exclusive fishery zone which has since been repealed by the Fishery Conservation and Management Act of 1976).  The United States and other "distant fishing" states continued to resist assertions of exclusive fishery jurisdiction beyond twelve miles.

Under the 1954 Fishermen's Protective Act, 22 U.S.C. §§ 1971 et seq., the United States reimburses United States flag vessels fined by foreign states for fishing in zones not recognized by the United States. This statute was amended in 1967 to provide for a reduction in financial assistance to countries which assessed such penalties against United States fishing vessels. 22 U.S.C. § 1975. See Meron, "The Fishermen's Protective Act: A Case Study in Contemporary Legal Strategy of the United States," 69 A.J.I.L. 290 (1975). Upon the adoption by the United States of a 200-mile fishery zone in 1976, the Fishery Conservation and Management Act amended the Fishermen's Protective Act, restricting its protection to seizures in circumstances other than those allowed under that Act for seizures of foreign vessels fishing in the United States fishery zone. 22 U.S.C. § 1972.

In 1972, Iceland established a 50-mile exclusive fishery zone, which was strongly contested by the United Kingdom and the Federal Republic of Germany who had historically fished in that area. The International Court of Justice recognized that a coastal state has preferential rights in the exploitation of fisheries in the seas around its coast, but that such preferential rights may not be exercised without taking into account the fishing rights of those states which have traditionally fished in the same waters and whose coastal communities depend on such fishing for their livelihood and economic well-being. The Court found that the governments were under mutual obligations to undertake negotiations in good faith for the equitable solution of their differences, taking into account both Iceland's preferential rights and the other states' established fishing rights in the areas. Fisheries Jurisdiction Cases (United Kingdom v. Iceland; Fed. Rep. of Germany v. Iceland), 1974 I.C.J. 3, 34; 175, 205–06.

The concept of a 200-mile zone in which a coastal state would have exclusive rights not only in relation to fisheries, but for the purpose of exploring, exploiting, and managing all of the living and nonliving natural resources therein was developed at the Third United Nations Conference on the Law of the Sea. See U.N. Doc. A/CONF./62/L.8/Rev.1 Annex II, at 3–4 (1971). While these negotiations were being conducted, several coastal states enacted unilaterally laws and regulations reserving exclusive rights in designated contiguous zones for the purpose of conservation, management and exploitation of all natural resources in waters contiguous to their territorial seas. See, for instance, the 1976 Fishery Conservation and Management Act, 16 U.S.C. §§ 1801–1882 (establishment of a 200-mile fishery conservation zone); the American Fisheries

Promotion Act of 1980, 94 Stat. 3299, 16 U.S.C. § 1821(e) (phase-out of foreign fishing within the 200-mile conservation zone); and the legislation of other nations in National Legislation and Treaties Relating to the Law of the Seas, U.N. Doc. ST/LEG/SER.B/18, at 271–377 (1976) and U.N. Doc. ST/LEG/SER.B/19, at 349–94 (1980).

Articles 55–75 of the LOS Convention establish a 200-mile zone in which a coastal state has not only sovereign rights for the purpose of exploring, exploiting, conserving and managing all the living resources therein, but also has such rights with respect to non-living resources of the seabed, its subsoil, and superjacent waters and other activities undertaken for the economic exploration and exploitation of the zone, such as the production of energy from the water, currents, and winds. Article 56. Within the EEZ, a coastal state has limited jurisdiction with regard to the establishment and use of artificial islands, installations and structures, marine scientific research and the protection and preservation of the marine environment. Id., Articles 56(1)(b) and 60, and Parts XII and XIII.

Within the E .Z, all states may exercise the high seas freedoms of navigation and overflight and of the laying of submarine cables and pipelines. They may also engage in other internationally lawful uses of the sea that are related to these freedoms, such as the operation of ships and aircraft.   Id., Article 58(1)–(2), with cross-references to Articles 87–115.   In exercising these freedoms, however, all states must give due regard to the rights and duties of the coastal state and shall comply with the lawful laws and regulations of the coastal state.   Id., Article 58(3).   Reciprocally, the coastal state must give due regard to the rights and duties of other states in exercising its rights and performing its duties in the EEZ.   Id., Article 56(2).

The broad consensus achieved at the Third Law of the Sea Conference and the practice of states have established as customary international law these general principles, and they are binding on states generally even before the Convention comes into effect.

On March 10, 1983, President Reagan issued Proclamation 5030, claiming a 200-mile EEZ in which the United States has rights and jurisdiction substantially similar to those of coastal states set forth in the LOS Convention.   48 Fed. Reg. 10605 (1983).   According to the statement of the President accompanying the Proclamation, the Proclamation is "consistent with those fair and balanced results in the Convention" which "generally confirm existing maritime law and practice."   22 I.L.M. 461, 464 (1983).

The United States and other major maritime states take the position that the EEZ continues to be a part of the high seas, although subject to special rights of the coastal states. Other states insist that the zone is a special zone of the coastal state subject to the freedoms of navigation and overflight. In view of the likely conflicts about this issue, it was agreed that such conflicts should be resolved on the basis of equity and in the light of all relevant circumstances, taking into account not only the respective importance of the interests of the states directly involved, but also the interests of the international community as a whole. LOS Convention, Article 59.

For further discussion of the development of the EEZ, see generally Krueger and Nordquist, "The Evolution of the 200-Mile Exclusive Economic Zone: State Practice in the Pacific Basin", 19 Va. J. Int'l L. 321 (1979); Comment, "Fishery and Economic Zones as Customary International Law," 17 San Diego L.Rev. 661 (1980).

## B. MANAGEMENT AND CONSERVATION OF THE LIVING RESOURCES WITHIN THE EEZ

The coastal state has two primary responsibilities in the management and conservation of the living resources within its EEZ. First, the coastal state is under a duty, taking into account the best scientific evidence available to it, to ensure through proper conservation and management measures that the living resources of the EEZ are not endangered by over-exploitation. LOS

Convention, Article 61(2). The coastal state must maintain or restore populations of harvested fisheries at levels which produce a "maximum sustainable yield." Id., Article 61(2)–(3). "Maximum sustainable yield" is the level of fishing of a stock of fish at which the maximum tonnage of fish can be harvested without depleting the stock. Though maximum sustainable yield is based primarily upon scientific and biological data, the coastal state must also take into account such factors as the economic needs of its coastal fishing communities, the special requirements of developing countries in the region, the effects on interrelated fishery stocks, fishing patterns, and any generally recommended international minimum standards. Id., Article 61(3)–(4). For a discussion of the development of the principle of "maximum sustainable yield," see Christy and Scott, The Common Wealth in Ocean Fisheries 215–42 (1965).

The second primary responsibility of the coastal state is to promote the objective of "optimum utilization" of the living resources within its EEZ, a more flexible concept than "full utilization." LOS Convention, Article 62(1). To this end, the coastal state shall determine the allowable catch of the living resources within its EEZ and its own capacity to harvest the allowable catch. Id., Articles 61(1) and 62(2). The coastal state's discretion in determining the allowable catch in its

EEZ is not prejudiced by its responsibility to promote optimum utilization. Id., Article 62(1). Therefore, a coastal state may set the entire allowable catch at a level equal to its capacity to harvest, even if such level is below the level which would ensure optimum utilization of fishery resources, thus cutting off access to foreign nations to any surplus which the coastal state cannot harvest. A coastal state may not, however, determine an allowable catch which would lead to over-exploitation of harvested species. Id., Article 61(2).

If a coastal state sets an allowable catch at levels above which the coastal state has the capacity to harvest, it must grant access to other states to harvest the available surplus. Id., Article 62(2). In granting access to other states, the coastal state must, among other considerations, give due regard to the rights and needs of land-locked states and geographically disadvantaged states in the region. Id., Article 62(2). This concession was granted to land-locked states and geographically disadvantaged states after protracted negotiations at the Third Law of the Sea Conference. No rights with respect to the exploitation of nonliving resources in the EEZ were granted to these states. For a more detailed presentation of the rights of land-locked and geographically disadvantaged states in the EEZ, see Section C, infra.

In addition to considering the rights and needs of land-locked and geographically disadvantaged states in the region, a coastal state in giving to other states access to its EEZ must take into account all relevant factors, including its own economic and other national interests, the requirements of developing states in the region, and the need to minimize economic dislocation in states whose nationals have habitually fished in the EEZ or which have made substantial efforts in research and identification of stocks in the EEZ. Id., Article 62(3).

Article 62(4) of the LOS Convention sets forth a non-exhaustive list of matters which a coastal state may regulate in its EEZ, including:

(a) the licensing of fishermen, fishing vessels and equipment and the payment of fees (see, e.g., 16 U.S.C. § 1824);

(b) establishing quotas and species which might be caught (see, e.g., the Atlantic Butterfish Management Plan, 50 C.F.R. § 657);

(c) regulation of seasons and areas of fishing, and the types, sizes and amount of gear and fishing vessels that may be used (see, e.g., the Atlantic Groundfish Management Plan, 50 C.F.R. § 651.22);

(d) the age and size of fish that may be caught (see, e.g., the Atlantic Herring Management Plan, 50 C.F.R. § 653.27);

(e) reporting requirements relating to fish caught (see, e.g., 50 C.F.R. § 611);

(f) fishery research programs (see, e.g., 15 U.S.C. § 713c–3(c));

(g) the placing of observers or trainees on foreign vessels (see, e.g., 16 U.S.C. § 1827);

(h) the landing of the catch by foreign vessels in the ports or waters of the coastal state (see, e.g., 16 U.S.C. § 1825);

(i) the terms of joint ventures;

(j) the training of personnel and transfer of fisheries technology; and

(k) enforcement procedures (see, e.g., 16 U.S.C. § 1861).

Where nationals of other states are granted access to a coastal state's EEZ, they must comply with the conservation measures and other lawful regulations and laws of the coastal state. LOS Convention, Articles 58(3) and 62(4).

For a study on the extent of a coastal state's legislation and regulation in the EEZ, see Part II of the U.N. Secretary-General's Study on the Future Functions of the Secretary-General under the Draft Convention and on the Needs of Countries, Especially Developing Countries, for Information, Advice and Assistance under the New Legal Regime, U.N. Doc. A/CONF.62/L. 76 (1981).

The LOS Convention provides that if a coastal state has neglected its duties under Articles 61 and 62 in some important respects, other states concerned may submit the matter to a compulsory conciliation procedure.  This procedure can be invoked in particular when:

> (a) a coastal state has manifestly failed to comply with its obligations to ensure through proper conservation and management measures that the maintenance of living resources in the exclusive economic zone is not seriously endangered;

> (b) a coastal state has arbitrarily refused to determine at the request of another State, the allowable catch and its capacity to harvest living resources with respect to stocks which that other state is interested in fishing;

> (c) a coastal state has arbitrarily refused to allocate to any State, the whole or part of the surplus it has declared to exist.

This procedure applies only in disputes between parties to the Convention, and cannot be invoked by the United States if it does not become a party to the Convention.  Article 297(3).

## C. RIGHTS OF GEOGRAPHICALLY DISAD-
## VANTAGED AND LAND–LOCKED
## STATES IN THE EEZ

Geographically disadvantaged states are coastal states which can claim no EEZ of their own and coastal states, including states bordering closed or semi-enclosed seas, whose geographical situations make them dependent upon the exploitation of the living resources of the EEZ of other coastal states in the region. LOS Convention, Article 70(2). These states include, for example, coastal states with a short coastline, such as Singapore or Zaire. Land-locked states are states which do not border open, enclosed or semi-enclosed seas. For a discussion of the criteria used in determining which states are geographically disadvantaged, and for listings of land-locked and geographically disadvantaged states, see Alexander & Hodgson, "The Role of the Geographically-Disadvantaged States in the Law of the Sea," 13 San Diego L. Rev. 558 (1976).

Land-locked states and geographically disadvantaged states have the right to participate, on an equitable basis, in the exploitation of any fishery surplus in the EEZs of coastal states in the region, taking into account the relevant economic and geographic circumstances of all the states concerned. LOS Convention, Articles 69(1) and 70(1). Developed land-locked and developed geographically disadvantaged states are entitled to participate only in the exploitation of surplus fisheries of the EEZs of other developed coastal states in the region, after the developed coastal state has given due regard to the need to minimize detrimental effects on states whose nationals have habitually fished in the zone. Id., Articles 69(4) and 70(5).

The terms of participation of geographically disadvantaged and land-locked states in a given EEZ shall be established by bilateral, subregional, or regional agreement. In establishing such terms, the states concerned must take into account the following factors:

   (a) the need to avoid effects detrimental to fishing communities or fishing industry of the coastal state;

   (b) the extent to which the land-locked or geographically disadvantaged state is participating or entitled to participate in the exploitation of other states' EEZs;

   (c) the need to avoid a particular burden for any single coastal state;  and

   (d) the nutritional needs of the populations of the states concerned.

Id., Articles 69(2) and 70(2).

When the harvesting capacity of a coastal state approaches a point which would enable it to harvest the entire allowable catch, the coastal state must cooperate in establishing equitable arrangements to allow the participation of developing land-locked and developing geographically disadvantaged states of the region in the exploitation of the living resources of the EEZ, as may be appropriate in the circumstances and on terms satisfactory to all parties concerned, taking into account the factors noted in the preceding paragraph. Id., Articles 69(3) and 70(4).

## D.  SPECIES SUBJECT TO SPECIAL RULES

Where the same stock of species occurs within the EEZs of two or more coastal states, or in an EEZ and an adjacent area of the high seas frequented by foreign fishermen, the states concerned must cooperate directly or through an international organization in enacting appropriate conservation and management measures. LOS Convention, Article 63. A similar duty is imposed regarding highly migratory species, such as tuna, which are listed in Annex I of the LOS Convention. Id., Article 64. The United States participates in several bilateral and multilateral treaties regarding these special species. See, for instance, the 1949 Convention for the Establishment of an Inter-American Tropical Tuna Commission; the 1952 International Convention for the High Seas Fisheries of the North Pacific Ocean; and the 1966 International Convention for the Conservation of Atlantic Tunas. With regard to the difficulties that have arisen with respect to migratory species, see Note, "The Tuna War: Fishery Jurisdiction in International Law," 1981 U.Ill.L.Rev. 755 (1981).

The exploitation of marine mammals in the EEZ may be more strictly regulated by the coastal state. LOS Convention, Article 65. The United States enacted a comprehensive protection plan for marine mammals in the Marine Mammal Protection Act of 1972, 16 U.S.C. §§ 1361–1362, 1371–1384, 1401–1407, and has also entered into numerous international agreements for the protection of marine mammals, such as the 1946 Whaling Convention.

With regard to anadromous and catadromous stocks, respectively, states in whose rivers these stocks originate or in which these stocks spend the greater part of their life cycle have the primary interest in and responsibility for such stocks. The coastal state must cooperate with other states whose nationals fish anadromous or catadromous stock outside the coastal state's EEZ, or with other states through whose waters these stocks migrate, and appropriate conservation and management measures should be enacted by agreement. In particular, arrangements are to be made to minimize economic dislocation for other states fishing these stocks. LOS Convention, Articles 66 and 67. For an example of such an agreement, see the 1930 Canada-United States Sockeye Salmon Fisheries Convention.

Coastal state management and exploitation of sedentary species are not governed by the provisions of the LOS Convention governing fisheries in the EEZ. LOS Convention, Article 68. Sedentary species are defined as organisms which, at the harvestable stage, either are immobile on or under the seabed or are unable to move except in constant physical contact with the seabed or the subsoil and are a part of the natural resources of the continental shelf. Id., Article 77. A coastal state's rights over sedentary species are discussed in Chapter VIII, Section D, infra.

## E. ENFORCEMENT OF CONSERVATION AND MANAGEMENT MEASURES

Within the EEZ, a coastal state has the right to enforce all laws and regulations enacted to conserve and manage living resources. LOS Convention, Article 73. The authorities of the coastal state, in enforcing such laws and regulations, may board and inspect a ship, arrest a ship and its crew, and institute judicial proceedings against them. Arrested ships and crews must be promptly released upon the posting of reasonable bond or other security. If such release is unduly delayed, and if the states concerned are parties to the Convention, an appeal may be made to the International Tribunal for the Law of the

Sea. Id., Articles 73(1)–(2) and 292. A coastal state's penalties may not include imprisonment or any other form of corporal punishment. Id., Article 73(3). But see 16 U.S.C. § 1859 which provides for imprisonment for violation of certain provisions of the Fishery Conservation and Management Act. The coastal state must inform the flag state of any vessel arrests or enforcement actions taken. LOS Convention, Article 73(4). The coastal state may engage in hot pursuit to arrest any ship which violates conservation or management measures within the coastal state's EEZ, provided such pursuit does not continue into the territorial waters of another state. Id., Article 111(2)–(3); United States v. F/V Taiyo Maru, 395 F.Supp. 413 (D.Me.1975).

Enforcement of regulations regarding anadromous species harvested beyond the EEZ requires an agreement between the coastal state and other states concerned. Similarly, enforcement of regulations regarding fishing of highly migratory species and straddling stocks harvested beyond the EEZ requires an agreement between all the states concerned. Id., Articles 63, 64 and 66. But see 16 U.S.C. §§ 1801(b)(1) and 1821(a) (U.S. enforcement authority over anadromous species extends through and beyond the 200-mile zone, except it shall not extend to such species while they are within a foreign fishery conservation zone); [1976] Digest of U.S. Practice in International Law 354–55.

## F. U. S. LEGISLATION RELATING TO CONSERVATION AND EXPLOITATION OF THE LIVING RESOURCES IN THE EEZ

The United States has always claimed exclusive sovereignty over the living (and non-living) resources in its territorial sea. See Chapter V. In 1966, Congress established a 9-mile fishery zone contiguous to the territorial sea in which the United States claimed exclusive fishing rights, subject to the continuation of fishing by states who had traditionally fished in those waters as recognized by the United States. 80 Stat. 908. This act did not establish a comprehensive program for the conservation or management of fisheries within the zone.

In 1976, Congress enacted the Fishery Conservation and Management Act, which extends United States fishery conservation and management jurisdiction over a newly established 200-mile fishery conservation zone. The legislation was enacted after a study conducted by the House Committee on Merchant Marine and Fisheries revealed, on the one hand, the overexploitation of certain fishery stocks in these waters, due primarily to foreign fishing activities, and, on the other hand, the relatively poor condition of the United States fishery fleet and industry. House Report No. 94–445, 94th Cong., 2d. Sess. 30–44 (1976), reprinted in [1976] U.S. Code Cong. & Adm. News 593, 602–12.

The Act specifies standards for the establishment of comprehensive conservation and management plans for each species of fishery stock within the 200-mile zone (other than highly migratory species), to be developed by regional fishery management councils. 16 U.S.C. §§ 1851–1855. The plans must prevent overexploitation of the fisheries within the zone and must promote on a continuing basis the harvest of an "optimum yield" from each fishery. 16 U.S.C. § 1851(a)(1). "Optimum yield" is defined as a yield which "will provide the greatest overall benefit to the Nation, with particular reference to food production and recreational opportunities," and which is determined "on the basis of the maximum sustainable yield from such fishery, as modified by any relevant economic, social, or ecological factor." 16 U.S.C. § 1802(18). In Maine v. Kreps, the court held that the Act did not preclude the selection of an optimum yield figure large enough to allow some foreign fishing, even though a lower figure would have rebuilt depleted fishery stocks more quickly. 563 F.2d 1043 (1st Cir. 1977).

In addition to establishing conservation and management authority in the zone, the Act established a system of controlling foreign access to the zone. The Act authorized foreign fishing within the zone only (1) if a treaty or international agreement currently in force so required access or (2) if the flag state entered "a governing international fishery agreement" with the United States acknowledging United States fishery conservation and management jurisdiction in the zone. 16 U.S.C. § 1821(a)–(b). Foreign vessels meeting either of these requirements may be issued a fishing permit only to harvest that portion of the "optimum yield" not harvested by United States fishermen. 16 U.S.C. § 1853(a)(4). The determination of optimum yield, United States harvest capacity, and the allocation of any surplus among foreign fishermen are the responsibilities of the regional councils.

The Fishery Conservation and Management Act provides for both civil and criminal penalties for violations of the Act. 16 U.S.C. §§ 1858–1859. The Act permits seizure of any fishing vessel violating the Act, but provides for a stay of execution upon payment of a bond. 16 U.S.C. § 1860(d). The Act also provides for revocation of fishing permits issued to foreign vessels which violate the Act. 16 U.S.C. § 1824(b)(12).

In United States v. Kaiyo Maru No. 53, 503 F. Supp. 1075 (D.Alaska 1980), the court upheld a warrantless search of a foreign fishing vessel under the Act and confirmed that under the Act all fish illegally caught must be forfeited. With regard to forfeiture of the vessel, the court disagreed with the government's contention that the vessel must also be forfeited, and relying on 16 U.S.C.

§ 1860(d) held that forfeiture of the foreign vessel was within the court's discretion and the court may permit any judgment to be recovered on the bond.

For discussions of the 1976 Act see Magnuson, "The Fishery Conservation and Management Act of 1976: First Step Toward Improved Management of Marine Fisheries", 52 Wash.L.Rev. 427 (1977); [1976] Digest of U.S. Practice in International Law 351–56.

In 1978 the Act was amended to promote the interests of United States processors by creating a priority in fishery resources in the zone for vessels which deliver their catch to United States processors. This legislation was intended to reverse the National Oceanic and Atmospheric Administration's decision that it had no authority under the 1976 Act to regulate joint ventures between United States fishing vessels and foreign processing vessels. 43 Fed.Reg. 20532 (1978). Permits for foreign processing vessels may be issued only for that portion of the optimum yield not utilized by United States processors. See Christie, "Regulation of International Joint Ventures in the Fishery Conservation Zone," 10 Ga.J.Int'l & Comp.L. 85 (1980).

The Act was further amended in 1980 to provide for complicated optional methods for determining the total allowable level of foreign fishing within the zone, which may result gradually in a total phase-out of foreign fishing within the zone. 16 U.S.C. § 1821(d). Until the phase-out is fully implemented, access to available surplus shall be allocated in part on a "market access" basis, giving preference to nationals of states which grant preferential access to their available surpluses to United States nationals. The rights of fishing vessels which have historically fished in the zone are another factor to be taken into account. 16 U.S.C. § 1821(e). See generally, House Report No. 96–1138, 96th Cong., 2d Sess., reprinted in [1980] U.S. Code Cong. & Admin. News 6869; Comment, "Fishery Conservation: Is the Categorical Exclusion of Foreign Fleets the Next Step?" 12 Cal.W.Int'l L.J. 154 (1982).

The Fishery Management and Conservation Act specifically excludes from United States fishery management authority highly migratory species such as tuna, reflecting the United States view that tuna management ought to be conducted by international agreement. 16 U.S.C. § 1813; see also 16 U.S.C. § 1801(b)(2), and the EEZ Proclamation, March 10, 1983, 48 Fed.Reg. 10605 (1983). The Act, however, expressly extends United States management and enforcement authority over anadromous species through and beyond the 200-mile zone, except that such management authority shall not extend to such species during the time they are found within any foreign nation's territorial sea or fishery conservation zone. 16 U.S.C. §§ 1801(b)(1) and 1821; see [1976]

Digest of U.S. Practice in International Law 354–55. For a discussion of the compatibility of the Act, as amended, with the LOS Convention, see Burke, "United States Fishery Management and the New Law of the Sea," 76 A.J.I.L. 24 (1982).

The Act preserves the jurisdiction of the coastal states of the United States over the territorial sea, including fishery management jurisdiction, so long as state jurisdiction relates to fishery stocks not predominantly fished beyond the territorial sea, and so long as any state actions do not adversely affect the fishery management plans adopted by the regional councils under the Act. 16 U.S.C. § 1856. The states are given an important role in the development of fishery conservation and management plans within the zone beyond the territorial sea by their representation on the eight regional fishery management councils set up under the Act. 16 U.S.C. § 1852. The federal government has enacted legislation to assist states in conserving and managing fisheries within their territorial seas, if they request such assistance. Coastal Zone Management Act of 1972, 16 U.S.C. §§ 1451–1464, as amended by 90 Stat. 1013 (1976) and 94 Stat. 2060 (1980).

According to Skiriotes v. Florida, a state may regulate fishing by its citizens on the high seas where there is no conflict with acts of Congress. 313 U.S. 69, 77 (1941). In People v. Weeren, the California Supreme Court held that California had jurisdiction to regulate fishing in the fishery conservation zone adjacent to California's territorial waters, since no federal rules had yet been promulgated under the 1976 Act. 26 Cal.3d 654, 163 Cal.Rptr. 255, 607 P.2d 1279 (1980).

Enactment of the Fishery Conservation and Management Act has been interpreted as reflecting the intent of Congress that the United States withdraw from the 1958 Fishing on the High Seas Convention. United States v. MYS Prokofyeva, 536 F.Supp. 793 (D.Alaska 1982). See also President Reagan's Proclamation 5030, establishing a 200-mile EEZ, 48 Fed.Reg. 10605 (1983), which appears to supersede the 1958 Convention.

## G. OTHER USES OF THE EXCLUSIVE ECONOMIC ZONE

In addition to the exploitation of the living resources of the EEZ, the coastal state may undertake other exploitation activities, such as the production of energy from the water, currents and winds. LOS Convention, Article 56. One area of activity which has been regulated by several states is the production of energy from the differentials in temperatures between the warm surface and the cooler subsurface waters of the ocean (ocean thermal energy conversion or "OTEC"). The electricity produced by the thermal energy may be transferred on-shore by submarine cables or may be used at the site of production to produce energy-intensive chemicals such as ammonia.

In 1980, Congress enacted the Ocean Thermal Energy Conversion Research and Development Act to promote the development of OTEC in the waters adjacent to the United States, 42 U.S.C. §§ 9001 et seq., and the Ocean Thermal Energy Conversion Act, to authorize and regulate the construction and operation of OTEC facilities in the territorial and adjacent waters of the United States, 42 U.S.C. §§ 9101 et seq. Only United States citizens, United States government entities, or corporations organized under the laws of any state of the United States with a United States chairman of the board and with at least a quorum of United States citizens as members may apply for a license under the Act. 42 U.S.C. §§ 9102 (18), 9111(f). Foreign vessels may not call at an OTEC facility unless its flag state has recognized United States jurisdiction over the vessel while within any safety zone which has been established around the facility. 42 U.S.C. § 9119 (b). Licensees must act in a manner that does not interfere with lawful uses of the high seas by other nations. 42 U.S.C. § 9119(a).

## H.   MARINE SCIENTIFIC RESEARCH

The coastal state has the right to regulate, authorize and conduct marine scientific research within its EEZ in accordance with the relevant provisions of the LOS Convention. Other states or international organizations may not conduct marine scientific research without the consent of the coastal state. Where the proposed research is to be conducted for peaceful purposes for the benefit of the scientific knowledge of all mankind, a coastal state may not withhold such consent, unless the proposed research is of direct significance for the exploration and exploitation of natural resources; involves drilling or the use of explosives or other harmful substances; involves the construction or use of artificial islands or structures; contains inaccurate information relating to the nature and objectives of the project; or if the applicant has outstanding obligations to the coastal state from a prior research project. LOS Convention, Article 246.

Other states or international organizations authorized to conduct marine scientific research may not unjustifiably interfere with a coastal state's lawful activities. Id., Article 246(8). The other state or international organization must provide certain information regarding the nature and objective of the project to the coastal state, and provide the coastal state with project reports and resulting data. Id., Articles 248 and 249(1). The other state or international organization must ensure the right of the coastal state, if it so desires, to participate or to be represented in the marine scientific research projects conducted in its EEZ, without payment of any remuneration to the scientists of the coastal state and without any obligation of the coastal state to contribute toward the costs of the project. Id., Article 249(1)(a). If the other state or international organization does not comply with these provisions, a coastal state may require the suspension of the project. Id., Article 253.

Between parties to the LOS Convention, disputes arising from the interpretation or application of these provisions shall be submitted to special conciliatory procedures. However, disputes involving the discretion of the coastal state to withhold its consent in accordance with Article 246 or to suspend a research project in accordance with Article 253 shall not be subject to dispute resolution. LOS Convention, Article 297(2).

In a statement accompanying Proclamation 5030, establishing a 200-mile EEZ for the United States (see Section A, supra), President Reagan specifically excluded any claim of jurisdiction on behalf of the United States over marine scientific research within the zone. 22 I.L.M. 461, 464 (1983).

## I.   ARTIFICIAL ISLANDS AND INSTALLATIONS

In the EEZ, the coastal state has the exclusive right to construct and regulate the construction, operation and use of any artificial islands, and of any installations and structures for economic purposes, provided that artificial islands, installations and structures may not be established where interference may be caused to the use of recognized sea lanes essential to international navigation.  LOS Convention, Article 60(1) and (7).

The coastal state has exclusive jurisdiction over such artificial islands, installations and structures, including jurisdiction with regard to customs, fiscal, health, safety, and immigration laws and regulations.  Id., Article 60(2).  Where necessary, the coastal state may establish safety zones not in excess of 500 meters around such artificial islands, installations and structures, and may take appropriate measures therein to ensure the safety of navigation and the structures themselves.  Id., Article 60(4)–(5).

Abandoned or disused installations or structures must be removed by the coastal state in a manner to ensure safety of navigation and in accordance with applicable international standards or regulations, and with due regard to fishing, the protection of the marine environment, and the rights and duties of other states.  Id., Article 60 (3).

In addition to their frequent use as deepwater ports and oil drilling rigs, artificial islands and similar structures have been proposed for numerous purposes including their use as locations for airports, nuclear power plants, broadcasting facilities, fish processing, and gambling resorts. See Note, "Jurisdictional Problems Created by Artificial Islands," 10 San Diego L.Rev. 638 (1973).

The Outer Continental Shelf Act of 1953, as amended, provides that the "Constitution and laws and civil and political jurisdiction of the United States are extended . . . to all artificial islands, and all installations and other devices permanently or temporarily attached to the seabed, which may be erected thereon for the purpose of exploring for, developing, or producing resources therefrom, or any such installation or other device (other than a ship or vessel) for the purpose of transporting such resources." 43 U. S.C. § 1333(a)(1). The Act further declares that the civil and criminal laws of each adjacent state, to the extent they are applicable and not inconsistent with the Act, shall constitute the laws of the United States with regard to such artificial islands and structures. 43 U.S.C. § 1333 (a)(2)(A).

The Coast Guard has the authority under the Act to make and enforce regulations with respect to lights, warning devices, safety equipment, and other safety matters on artificial islands and installations. 43 U.S.C. § 1333(d)(1). The Coast Guard must require on all drilling and production operations begun after 1978, and wherever practicable regarding installations constructed earlier, the use of the best available and safest technologies which are economically feasible. 43 U.S.C. § 1347(b). For the safety regulations promulgated by the Coast Guard, see 33 C.F.R. Part 140. Under the Act, the Department of Labor's authority to regulate labor conditions is acknowledged. 43 U.S.C. § 1347(d). However, where safety and health regulations overlap, and the Coast Guard first exercises its authority, the authority of the Department of Labor is displaced. Marshall v. Nichols, 486 F.Supp. 615 (D.C.Tex.1980).

The Secretary of the Army has authority to prevent an obstruction to navigation which may be caused by artificial islands, installations or structures. 43 U.S.C. § 1333(e). For regulations establishing a 500-meter safety zone around artificial islands, installation, and structures, see 33 C.F.R. §§ 147.1–.15 (1982). For the regulation of navigation around artificial islands and similar installations, see 33 C.F.R. Part 67.

Where there is a gap in federal law or where applicable state law does not conflict with federal law, the law of the state adjacent to the continental shelf becomes the law of the United States to be applied to artificial islands and installations. Oliver v. Aminoil, U.S.A., Inc., 662 F.2d 349 (5th Cir. 1981) (under applicable Louisiana law platform owner was not liable for personal injuries of employee of another without showing fault). See Note, "The Application of Louisiana's Strict Liability Law on the Outer Continental Shelf: A Quandary for Federal Courts," 28 Loyola L.Rev. 101 (1982). State and federal courts have concurrent jurisdiction over claims of action arising under the Act. Gulf Offshore Co. v. Mobil Oil Corp., 453 U.S. 473 (1981). See Note, "State Court Jurisdiction Under the Outer Continental Shelf Lands Act," 28 Loyola L.Rev. 343 (1982).

The Deepwater Port Act of 1974, 33 U.S.C. §§ 1501 et seq., establishes the legal framework for licensing the construction and operation of port facilities in waters beyond the United States territorial limits for facilitation of tanker and supertanker traffic. The Secretary of Transportation has issued regulations governing the issuance of construction licenses, pollution prevention, safety, navigation, operations and enforcement. 33 C.F.R. §§ 148.400–407. Subject to recognized principles of international law, safety zones may be established on a port-by-port basis. 33 U.S.C. § 1509(d). See, e.g., 33 C.F.R. Part 150, Appendix A. The Act does not apply to ports constructed in connection with offshore drilling platforms and used exclusively for storage and shipment of oil or gas produced there. Get Oil Out! Inc. v. Exxon Corp., 586 F.2d 726 (9th Cir. 1978).

Except in a situation involving force majeure, a foreign flag vessel may not utilize a deepwater port unless its flag state has recognized the jurisdiction of the United States over the vessel and its personnel while at the deepwater port and while in any authorized safety zones. 33 U.S.C. § 1518(c). See e.g., 1979 United States-United Kingdom Offshore Oil Ports Agreement.

# CHAPTER VIII

# CONTINENTAL SHELF

## A. EARLY DEVELOPMENTS

The rights of states in the seabed and its subsoil was an issue first raised primarily in the context of the right to exploit sedentary fisheries. In his pioneering article, "Whose is the Bed of the Sea," 4 Brit.Y.B. Int'l L. 34 (1923), Sir Cecil Hurst, after surveying the practices of several states, concluded that a state could acquire rights of sovereignty in the seabed adjacent to it where the state effectively and continuously occupied the seabed for a long period of time. Such occupation could be demonstrated through exclusive exploitation of sedentary species such as pearls, oysters, sponges or coral. Such ownership could not conflict with the freedom of navigation of the superjacent waters nor with the common right of the public to fish non-sedentary species in the area.

In 1945, President Truman issued two proclamations, one pertaining to fisheries in the high seas contiguous to the territorial sea of the United States (see Chapter VII, Section A) and the second pertaining to the natural resources of the subsoil and seabed of the continental shelf adjacent to the United States. In his Continental

[*150*]

Shelf Proclamation, President Truman stated that in view of the "long range worldwide need for new sources of petroleum and other minerals . . . the Government of the United States regards the natural resources of the subsoil and sea bed of the continental shelf beneath the high seas but contiguous to the coasts of the United States as appertaining to the United States, subject to its jurisdiction and control. . . . The character as high seas of the waters above the continental shelf and the right to their free and unimpeded navigation are in no way thus affected." 10 Fed.Reg. 12303 (1945).

The Truman Proclamation has been acknowledged by the International Court of Justice as being "the starting point of the positive law on the subject [of the continental shelf.]" North Sea Continental Shelf Cases (Fed. Rep. of Germany-Denmark and The Netherlands), 1969 I.C.J. 3, 32–33. Though the Proclamation did not actually claim sovereignty over the continental shelf, but only stated the United States policy regarding the natural resources of the subsoil and seabed of the continental shelf, it prompted numerous claims of sovereignty over the continental shelf, its seabed and subsoil, its superjacent waters and, in some instances, the overlying airspace. These claims were made primarily by Latin American states; see, for example, the 1946 Argentine Decree, Laws and Regulations on the Regime of the High Seas, U.N. Doc. ST/LEG./SER.B/1, at 4–5 (1951). Since many of the Latin American states do not have extensive continental shelves, they asserted sovereignty over a stated distance, usually 200 miles, with an emphasis on fisheries within that zone. See, e.g., 1947 Chile Decree, id. at 6–7. The United States protested both types of these extensive claims of sovereignty. 4 Whiteman, Digest of International Law 793–802 (1965).

In 1953, the United States enacted the Outer Continental Shelf Lands Act to regulate the exploration and exploitation of the continental shelf. 43 U.S.C. §§ 1331 et seq. (See Section F, infra.) Other nations also enacted laws regulating activities on the continental shelf. See, e.g., Australia, Pearl Fisheries Act and Regulations of 1952–54, Supplement to Laws and Regulations on the Regime of the High Seas, U.N. Doc. ST/LEG./SER.B/8, at 4, 8 (1959).

In 1958, a Convention on the Continental Shelf was concluded at the First United Nations Conference on the Law of the Sea. The Convention embodies the principle of sovereign rights of the coastal state over the continental shelf for the purpose of exploring its seabed and subsoil and exploiting its natural resources. Article 2. These rights do not affect the legal status of the superjacent waters as high seas, and their exercise may not unjustifiably interfere with the exercise of the high seas freedoms by other states. Id., Articles 3 and 5(1). These principles have been incorporated into the LOS Convention, and in some instances have been refined and expanded. In addition, the LOS Convention imposes some duties on the coastal state in favor of other states and the international community. Articles 76–85. The rights and duties of coastal states relating to the continental shelf are discussed in Section C, infra.

## B. DEFINITION AND DELIMITATION

The term "continental shelf" apparently was first used in a geological and geographical context in the late nineteenth century. As shown in the illustration, infra, the continental shelf is known, geologically, as those submarine areas which extend from the shore to the point at which there is a marked fall-off (the continental slope) to the ocean floor of the deep seabed.

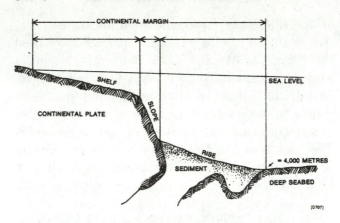

**Illustration 6**

The breadth of the continental shelf varies greatly among various regions. Several Latin American states bordering on the Pacific, for example, have narrow continental shelves while other states, such as the Latin American states bordering the Atlantic, have much wider continental shelves.

The term "continental shelf" acquired legal significance after its use in the Truman Proclamation and in other similar decrees issued shortly thereafter by various states. The Proclamation did not define "continental shelf," but in an accompanying press release it was generally considered to be the subsoil and seabed of the submarine areas contiguous to the coasts of the United States and covered by no more than 100 fathoms (600 feet or 200 meters) of water.

Article 1 of the 1958 Convention on the Continental Shelf defines the "continental shelf" as "the seabed and subsoil of the submarine areas adjacent to the coast [including the coast of islands] but outside the area of the territorial sea, to a depth of 200 meters or, beyond that limit, to where the depth of the superjacent waters admits of the exploitation of the natural resources of the said areas." This definition, which was formulated only after much study and debate, adopts two criteria. The first criterion, the 200-meter limit, is based upon a very general approximation of the point at which the continental shelf normally ends. In fact, the increase in slope marking the edge of the continental shelf is known to occur at less than 150 meters and more than 400 meters. The use of the 200-meter limit was regarded as necessary to provide uniformity and certainty to the concept of the continental shelf. The second criterion, exploitability, assured the right of coastal states to exploit natural resources of the seabed beyond the 200-meter mark in the event that technologies were improved to permit such exploitation in the future. See Report of the International Law Commission, U.N. Doc. A/3159, [1956] 2 Y.B. Int'l Law Comm'n 253, 296–97; Gutteridge, "The 1958 Geneva Convention on the Continental Shelf," 35 Brit. Y.B. Int'l L. 102 (1959).

The delegates to the Third United Nations Conference on the Law of the Sea found the definition of continental shelf embodied in the 1958 Convention on the Continental Shelf to be unsatisfactory. In particular, coastal states desired to extend their sovereignty over a wider belt of the continental shelf in view of technological advances making such areas exploitable. The exploitability criterion of the 1958 definition was regarded as too imprecise and unclear, and the 200-meter criterion was an overbroad generalization which did not relate to the concept of the continental shelf as an extension of the land mass of the coastal state. The delegates also recognized that a new definition of the continental shelf would have to be compatible with the concept of a 200-mile exclusive economic zone. The delegates endorsed the International Court of Justice's holding in the North Sea Continental Shelf Cases (Fed. Rep. of Germany—Denmark and The Netherlands), 1969 I.C.J. 3, 31, that the continental shelf is a natural prolongation of the land mass of the adjacent coastal state and based their new definition of the continental shelf upon that concept. See generally, the discussion in the Second Committee, 2 UNCLOS III, Off. Rec. 142–69, 171 (1974).

The LOS Convention expands the definition of the continental shelf to include "the seabed and subsoil of the submarine areas that extend beyond its territorial sea throughout the natural prolongation of its land territory to the outer edge of the continental margin, or to a distance of 200 nautical miles from the baselines from which the breadth of the territorial sea is measured where the outer edge of the continental margin does not extend up to that distance." LOS Convention, Article 76(1). Where the outer edge of continental margin (which term includes not only the continental shelf, but its subsequent slope and rise) extends beyond 200 miles, the coastal state may determine its continental shelf by using either (1) a line drawn by reference to points no more than 60 nautical miles from the foot of the slope, or (2) a line drawn by reference to points at which the thickness of sediments is less than 1 percent of the distance to the base of the continental slope. Id., Article 76(4). However, in no event may the outer limit of the shelf exceed 350 nautical miles from the baseline of the territorial sea or 100 nautical miles from the 2500 meter isobath (a line connecting points where the waters are 2500 meters deep). Id., Article 76(5). On submarine ridges, other than "submarine elevations that are natural components of the continental margin, such as its plateaux, rises, caps, banks and spurs," only the 350-mile limit applies.

Id., Article 76(6). See generally, Emery, "Geological Limits of the 'Continental Shelf'," 10 Ocean Development & Int'l L.J. 1 (1981).

In view of the complexity of these provisions, a special Commission on the Limits of the Continental Shelf will be established, and the limits are to be determined in cooperation between the coastal state and the Commission through a multi-step procedure. LOS Convention, Article 76(8) and Annex II.

As defined by the LOS Convention, and as now accepted by customary international law, there are in effect two continental shelves. The first corresponds with the geological definition of continental shelf and extends to the outer edge of the continental margin. The second is purely legal and corresponds with the coastal state's 200-mile EEZ (whether or not the coastal state's geological continental shelf in fact extends that far). Since the coastal state's jurisdiction in its EEZ includes rights to the resources of the underlying seabed and subsoil, the doctrine of the continental shelf grants important additional rights only in those areas of the continental shelf which extend beyond 200 nautical miles. However, even within the EEZ, the doctrine of the continental shelf grants some additional rights to the coastal state. For example, in contrast to its rights relating to EEZ fisheries, the coastal state is not required to conserve or share the natural resources of the continental shelf, including sedentary fisheries. See Sections C and D, infra.

Where the coastal state does have a continental shelf which extends beyond 200 nautical miles, its rights and duties in that area vary in some important respects from its rights and duties on the continental shelf within the 200-mile zone. For example, see Section C, infra, relating to exploitation of non-living resources beyond 200 miles by parties to the LOS Convention, and Section E, infra, relating to marine scientific research.

## C. RIGHTS AND DUTIES OF THE COASTAL STATE OVER THE CONTINENTAL SHELF

The coastal state has sovereign rights over the continental shelf for the purpose of exploring it and exploiting its natural resources. The rights of the coastal state do not depend upon actual exploration, exploitation, or other assertion of the right. In the event the coastal state does not exercise its rights, no one else may explore or exploit its continental shelf without the express consent of the coastal state. 1958 Convention on the Continental Shelf, Article 2; LOS Convention, Articles 77 and 81. See United States v. Ray, 423 F.2d 16 (5th Cir. 1970) (consent of the United States required to construct man-made island upon coral reefs located on the continental shelf).

The coastal state does not have sovereign rights over the continental shelf for purposes other than the exploration or exploitation of its natural resources. Treasure Salvors, Inc. v. Unidentified Wrecked and Abandoned Sailing Vessel, 569 F.2d 330 (5th Cir. 1978) (United States jurisdiction under the Outer Continental Shelf Act as modified by the 1958 Convention on the Continental Shelf does not extend to non-resource related material in the shelf area and does not cover objects such as wrecked ships and their cargoes lying on or under the seabed).

Natural resources are defined as the mineral and other non-living resources of the seabed and subsoil, and sedentary fisheries (organisms which are, at the harvestable stage, either immobile on or under the seabed or unable to move except in constant physical contact with the seabed or the subsoil). 1958 Convention on the Continental Shelf, Article 2(4); LOS Convention, Article 77 (4). See Section D, infra, regarding sedentary fisheries. The Submerged Land Act of 1953 defines "natural resources" to include (without limiting the generality thereof) "oil, gas, and all other minerals, and fish, shrimp, oysters, clams, crabs, lobsters, sponges, kelp, and other marine animal and plant life but does not include water power, or the use of water for the production of power." 43 U.S.C. § 1301(e). In United States v. Ray, 423 F.2d 16, 21–22 (5th Cir. 1970), the court held that coral reefs and their coral and pescatorial inhabitants are "natural resources" as defined by the Act and the 1958 Convention on the Continental Shelf.

The rights of the coastal state over the continental shelf do not affect the legal status of the superjacent waters and airspace. In exercising its rights, the coastal state may not infringe upon or unjustifiably interfere with navigation and the other high seas freedoms of overflight, of fishing, to lay submarine cables and pipelines, and to conduct scientific research. 1958 Convention on the Continental Shelf, Articles 3 and 5(1); LOS Convention, Articles 78 and 87. The coastal state may, however, take reasonable measures to prevent and control pollution from pipelines, and the delineation of the course of a pipeline is subject to the coastal state's consent. Cables or pipelines constructed for the exploitation or exploration of the natural resources of the continental shelf or for the use in artificial islands, installations and structures on the continental shelf or in the EEZ are subject to the coastal state's jurisdiction, as are cables and pipelines which enter the coastal state's territorial sea. LOS Convention, Article 79.

Other states may not drill on the continental shelf without the coastal state's consent for any purpose, including the exercise of high seas freedoms such as scientific research. Id., Article 81.

Article 60 of the LOS Convention governing artificial islands, installations and structures in the EEZ applies *mutatis mutandis* to artificial islands, installations, and structures on the continental shelf. See Chapter VII, Section I, supra.

The LOS Convention imposes certain obligations upon parties to the Convention with regard to the exploitation of the non-living resources of the continental shelf beyond 200 miles from the baseline from which the territorial sea is measured. The coastal state (except for certain developing states) must make payments or contributions in kind annually after the first five years of production occurring at a site beyond the 200-mile zone. In the sixth year, the coastal state shall pay 1 percent of the value or volume of production at the site, which rate increases each year until it reaches 7 percent. The graduated rate structure is intended to permit the coastal state to recoup start-up costs before having to make the payments or contributions. The term "production" does not include resources used in connection with the exploitation. LOS Convention, Article 82.

The payments or contributions in kind shall be made to the Authority established to regulate and govern deep seabed mining (see Chapter IX, infra). The Authority will distribute the payments or contributions to states which are parties to the Convention on an equitable sharing basis, taking into account the interests and needs of developing states, particularly the least developed states and land-locked states. Id.

The regime established in Article 82 is not binding upon states not parties to the Convention. For a statement of the United States position, see [1976] Digest of U.S. Practice in International Law 345.

## D. SEDENTARY FISHERIES

The coastal state has sovereign rights over the sedentary fisheries of its continental shelf. 1958 Convention on the Continental Shelf, Article 2(4); LOS Convention, Article 77. In contrast to its obligations within the EEZ, the coastal state is not obligated to manage and conserve its sedentary fisheries to provide for an "optimum yield," nor must the coastal state grant access to any portion of its sedentary fisheries to other states. LOS Convention, Article 68.

At the First United Nations Conference on the Law of the Sea, the drafting of a definition of "continental shelf resources" was highly controversial. 4 Whiteman, Digest of International Law 856–64 (1965). As finally drafted (see Section C, supra), it was not clear whether certain species of crustacea and other organisms fell within the definition. In 1960, the United States Department of State stated that "clams, oysters, abalone, etc. are included in the definition, whereas shrimp, lobsters, and finny fish are not." Hearing on the Law of the Sea Conventions before the Committee on Foreign Relations, U.S. Senate, 86th Cong., 2d Sess. at 82, 88 (1960). In 1964, Congress enacted the Bartlett Act, 78 Stat. 194 (superseded in 1976 by the Fishery Conservation and Management Act), which prohibited foreign vessels from taking any "Continental Shelf fishery resource." The Secretary of the Interior was authorized to list those species covered by the term. Japan protested against the inclusion of Alaskan king crab within the definition, asserting that they are a high seas fishery resource. 4 Whiteman, Digest of International Law 864–65 (1965). Similarly, France protested Brazil's assertion of jurisdiction over lobsters, id. at 864, and other protests have been made by various states regarding a coastal state's exercise of jurisdiction over various species. Generally, the coastal state has prevailed.

The conservation and management of sedentary fisheries located on the United States continental shelf are governed by the Fishery Conservation and Management Act of 1976, as amended, 16 U.S.C. §§ 1801 et seq. The term "continental shelf" has not been amended to reflect the newly established definition in the LOS Convention, but reiterates the 1958 Convention on the Continental Shelf definition. The term "Continental Shelf fishery resources" is defined to include several species of coral, crustacea (including crab and lobster), abalone, conch, clams, and sponges. The Secretary of Commerce is authorized to include other species within the term by regulation. 16 U.S.C. § 1802(4).

## E. MARINE SCIENTIFIC RESEARCH ON THE CONTINENTAL SHELF

The provisions of the LOS Convention governing marine research in the EEZ apply to marine research on the continental shelf. Articles 246–55. See Chapter VII, Section H, supra. However, beyond 200 nautical miles, the coastal state may not exercise its discretion to withhold consent on the basis that a proposed research project has direct significance for the exploration or exploitation of natural resources, if research is to be conducted in areas other than those in which the coastal state has begun exploitation or detailed exploratory operations or in which it will begin such operations within a reasonable period of time. Id., Article 246(6).

## F. UNITED STATES PRACTICE AND LEGISLATION RELATING TO THE CONTINENTAL SHELF

After issuance of the Truman Proclamation, disputes arose among the states and the federal government over the rights of each in the natural resources of the continental shelf. Many states enacted legislation establishing a regulatory system for the leasing, exploration and exploitation of the natural resources of the continental shelf in the territorial sea adjacent to their coasts. The United States instituted several actions to enjoin the states from implementing these regulatory schemes, and to claim ownership of the natural resources of the continental shelf in these areas. In 1947, the United States Supreme Court held that the United States was "possessed of paramount rights in, and full dominion and power over, the lands, minerals and other things" underlying the waters seaward of the low-water mark and outside of the inland waters of the coastal states, and that the coastal states had "no title thereto or property interest therein." United States v. California, 332 U.S. 19 (1947), and Decree, 332 U.S. 804, 805 (1947). The principle of federal sovereignty over the natural resources of the continental shelf was applied again in United States v. Louisiana, 339 U.S. 699 (1950) and Decree, 340 U.S. 899 (1950), and in United States v. Texas, 339 U.S. 707 (1950) and Decree, 340 U.S. 900 (1950).

In 1953, Congress enacted the Outer Continental Shelf Lands Act (OCSLA) which established a regulatory system for the leasing, exploration and exploitation of the non-living resources of the continental shelf beyond three miles (or nine miles in certain historic cases) from the baseline from which the territorial sea is measured. 43 U.S.C. §§ 1331 et seq. The simultaneously enacted Submerged Lands Act relinquished all rights, title and interest of the United States in the continental shelf and its resources within three miles of the baseline (or within nine miles in certain historic cases) to the adjacent states. 43 U.S.C. §§ 1301 et seq. The United States reserved its powers of regulation and control in those areas for purposes of commerce, navigation, national defense, and international affairs, and specifically reserved its rights in and title to the continental shelf seaward of the conceded areas. 43 U.S.C. § 1314.

In United States v. States of Louisiana, Texas, Mississippi, Alabama, and Florida, 363 U.S. 1 (1959), and United States v. Florida, id. at 121, the Supreme Court found that, based upon historic circumstances, the relevant boundary for Texas and the Gulf side of Florida for purposes of the Submerged Lands Act extended to a distance of three marine leagues (nine miles) beyond the baseline. The other states were entitled only to those lands, minerals and other natural resources underlying the Gulf to a distance of three geographical miles of the baseline.

The OCSLA established very general guidelines and directives for the Secretary of the Interior in managing the resources of the "outer continental shelf" (the continental shelf beyond the areas conceded to the states) and in leasing tracts for oil, gas and other mineral exploration and development. The Secretary was authorized to grant oil and gas leases on tracts not exceeding 5,760 acres (3 miles by 3 miles) for a period of five years and for as long thereafter as approved by the Secretary. Leases were to be granted by competitive bidding on the basis of a cash bonus with a fixed royalty. Under this system, whoever offered the most "front end" money was awarded the lease. 43 U.S.C. § 1337 (1964). Other than providing this skeletal framework, the OCSLA granted the Secretary broad discretion in structuring and implementing the Act.

The increased need for exploration and exploitation of continental shelf resources resulting from the oil shortage of the 1970's produced dissatisfaction, primarily from the states and environmental groups, with the over-general directives of the OCSLA. The OCSLA was amended in 1978 to establish a comprehensive national policy for continental shelf exploration and exploitation, to revise the federal leasing system significantly, to provide coastal states with an increased role in federal exploration and exploitation decisions on the continental shelf beyond state boundaries, to provide for safety standards on off-shore installations and other exploration and exploitation operations, to enhance environmental protection, and to establish an oil spill liability fund. 43 U.S.C. §§ 1331–1356.

Under the 1978 amendments, alternative bidding systems other than cash bonus bidding "shall be applied to not less than 20 per centum and not more than 60 per centum of the total area offered" for a five-year period following enactment of the amendments. 43 U.S.C. § 1337 (a)(5)(B). Six alternative methods are set forth in the amendments, and the Secretary of the Interior is authorized to use others. 43 U.S.C. § 1337(a)(1)(A)–(H).

The Secretary must prepare and periodically revise a five-year schedule of proposed oil and gas lease sales, taking into account a list of designated factors intended to ensure a proper balance among the disparate concerns involved. 43 U.S.C. § 1334(a). To ensure that the Secretary takes into account all relevant policy considerations, the 1978 amendments provide for participation by affected state and local governments, relevant federal agencies and the public. 43 U. S.C. § 1344. When the states of Alaska and California challenged the 1980–85 oil and gas lease plan prepared by the Secretary of the Interior, the court found much of the Secretary's program free from fault, but held that he erred in several regards, including a failure "to strike a proper balance incorporating environmental and coastal zone factors and not simply administrative need and economic factors such as potential oil and gas recovery." California v. Watt, 668 F.2d 1290, 1325 (D.C.Cir.1981). The plan was remanded to

the Secretary for revision.  The revised plan for
1982–87 set forth a leasing program which would
offer, in 41 oil and gas lease sales, almost all of
the one billion acres comprising the United States
OCS.  The revised plan has been upheld.  California v. Watt, 712 F.2d 584 (D.C.Cir.1983).

In 1981, the Secretary of the Interior announced an OCS lease sale of the entire Santa
Maria basin offshore a scenic stretch of coastline extending from Big Sur to Santa Barbara.
The lease sale was enjoined in an action brought
by California, which demanded a showing that
the lease sales would be consistent with its coastal
zone management program pursuant to Section
307 of the Coastal Zone Management Act, 16
U.S.C. § 1456(c)(1).  The United States Supreme
Court held that lease sales on the OCS are not
activities "directly affecting" the coastal zone
and therefore need not be shown to be consistent
with a state's management plan.  Secretary of
the Interior v. California, 104 S.Ct. 656 (1984).

Environmental impact studies must be prepared
for each area included in any oil and gas lease
sale and must be submitted for pubic review.  43
U.S.C. § 1346.  Inadequate environmental impact
statements have been the basis for several suits
challenging oil and gas lease sale programs.  See,
e.g., Natural Resources Defense Council, Inc. v.
Morton, 458 F.2d 827 (D.C.Cir. 1972) (environmental impact statement relating to oil and gas

lease sale off the coast of Louisiana was inadequate due to failure to discuss the environmental risks incident to alternative energy sources).

Where a proposed lease area underlies both the outer continental shelf and the continental shelf seaward of the territorial sea, the adjacent state is entitled to enter an agreement to permit an equitable division of any resulting revenues. 43 U.S.C. § 1337(g).

For a detailed discussion of the 1978 amendments, see Jones, "The Legal Framework for Energy Development on the Outer Continental Shelf," 10 UCLA-Alaska L.Rev. 143 (1981).

For regulations of the Secretary of the Interior governing the leasing, exploration and exploitation of the continental shelf resources, see 30 C.F.R. Part 250.

For a discussion of the strict safety and health standards required to be imposed on all outer continental shelf exploration and exploitation operations and their enforcement, see Chapter VII, Section I.

For a discussion of the establishment of an Offshore Oil Pollution Compensation Fund to be financed by a fee imposed on each barrel of oil produced on the outer continental shelf and the liability of owners and operators of offshore installations for environmental damage, see Chapter X, infra.

# CHAPTER IX

# EXPLOITATION OF THE MINERAL RESOURCES OF THE DEEP SEABED

## A. CURRENT STATUS OF THE LEGAL REGIME OF THE DEEP SEABED

A universally recognized legal regime governing the exploitation of the mineral resources of the deep seabed beyond the zones of national jurisdiction does not exist at the present time. While the doctrine of the continental shelf emerged and was acknowledged as customary international law at the First United Nations Conference of the Law of the Sea (see Chapter VIII), the general belief that the exploration and exploitation of the seabed and subsoil beyond national jurisdiction would not be technologically possible in the near future precluded serious consideration of the issue at that time. See the comments of the Special Rapporteur of the International Law Commission on "The Régime of the High Seas and Régime of the Territorial Sea," U.N. Doc. A/CONF.4/97 (1956), [1956] 2 Y.B. Int'l L. Comm'n 1, 9 and the comments of the United States delegate at 6 UNCLOS I, Off.Rec. 40 (1958).

Vast mineral resources in the form of "manganese nodules" were discovered on the deep ocean floors in the 1960's, and technological advances made exploitation of the nodules appear economically feasible. (In addition to manganese, the nodules contain other important minerals, including nickel, copper, and cobalt.) These developments brought the issue of the legal status of the deep seabed to the international forefront, and three divergent views regarding the legal status of the deep seabed have developed.

One view, adhered to primarily by the developing states, asserts that the mineral resources of the deep seabed are the common heritage of mankind (*res communis*) and may be exploited only by or under the auspices of an international authority acting on behalf of all countries. Until the establishment of such an authority, no state or person may claim, explore, or exploit these resources. This view was embodied in the Moratorium Resolution passed by the United Nations General Assembly in 1969, which prohibited deep seabed exploitation activities (but not exploration). The vote was 62 in favor, 28 against (including the United States and most other developed nations), with 28 abstentions. Resolution 2574–D, U.N. G.A.O.R., Supp. No. 30, at 11, U.N. Doc. A/7630 (1969).

A second view, adhered to by the United States and many other developed nations, defines the exploration and exploitation of mineral resources of the deep seabed as a freedom of the high seas.

Under this view, no state may claim or acquire sovereign or exclusive rights over any part of the deep seabed or its mineral resources. However, unless or until a state agrees to be bound otherwise, it may authorize or engage in the exploration and exploitation of deep seabed mineral resources, provided that such activities are conducted with reasonable regard for the rights of other states or persons to engage in similar activities and to exercise the freedoms of the high seas. See, e.g., the 1980 Deep Seabed Hard Mineral Resources Act, 30 U.S.C. §§ 1401(12) and 1402(a) (2).

A third view proposed by some legal scholars argues that the deep seabed, like unclaimed land, belongs to no one (*res nullius*) and may be appropriated to the exclusion of all others by the first nation which claims and exploits a particular area of the seabed. See, e.g., Goldie, "Customary International Law and Deep Seabed Mining," 6 Syracuse J. Int'l L. & Com. 173 (1978–79).

For a thorough discussion of these divergent views and their legal premises, see Van Dyke and Yuen, " 'Common Heritage' v. 'Freedom of the High Seas': Which Governs the Seabed?", 19 San Diego L.Rev. 493 (1982).

In 1970, the United Nations General Assembly adopted by a unanimous vote (including the United States and most developed nations) with 14 abstentions the "Declaration of Principles Governing the Sea-Bed . . . Beyond the Limits of National Jurisdiction." Resolution 2749 (XXV), 25 U.N. G.A.O.R. Supp. No. 28, at 24, U.N. Doc. A/8028 (1970). The Declaration states that the deep seabed and its natural resources "are the common heritage of mankind," and that the exploitation of its resources shall be carried out for the benefit of mankind as a whole, taking into particular consideration the interests and needs of the developing countries. The Declaration provides that all activities regarding the exploration and exploitation of the resources of the deep seabed shall be governed by an international regime to be established under a generally accepted international treaty of a universal character based upon the principles of the Declaration.

The Declaration does not expressly forbid or authorize the exploration for and the exploitation of the mineral resources of the deep seabed pending the establishment of a generally accepted international treaty of a universal character. The United States and several other nations made statements, at the time of its adoption, that the Declaration was not binding and did not constitute an interim deep seabed mining regime. U.N. Doc. A/C.1/PV.1799, at 1, 3–4 (1970). In particular, the United States rejected the earlier Moratorium Resolution and reserved its right to begin exploration and exploitation of the deep seabed on a nonexclusive basis with regard to the rights of other states until it becomes a party to an international agreement establishing a new international regime.   Id.

The Declaration served as a basis for negotiating an international regime for the exploration and exploitation of the deep seabed at the Third United Nations Conference on the Law of the Sea. The United States participated actively in the negotiations.   See the United States Draft United Nations Convention on the International Seabed Area, U.N. Doc. A/AC.138/25, in 25 U.N. G.A.O.R., Supp. No. 21, at 130, U.N. Doc. A/8021 (1970).   After delaying the adoption of several legislative proposals establishing a framework authorizing and regulating the exploration and exploitation of the deep seabed by United States citizens, in the hope of negotiating an acceptable regime at UNCLOS III, the United States adopted in 1980 the Deep Seabed Hard Mineral Resources Act.   30 U.S.C. §§ 1401 et seq.   The Act was based on findings that the UNCLOS III negotiations may not be concluded in the near future and, pending the ratification of a Law of the Sea Treaty by the United States, it was necessary to establish an interim deep seabed mining regime to encourage the continued development of deep seabed mining technology, which would result in benefits to mankind as a whole.   30 U.S.C. § 1401(a).   The Act was intended to be transitional until the entry into force with respect to the United States of the LOS Convention or, if such adoption is not forthcoming, until the adoption of other bilateral or multilateral treaties. 30 U.S.C. § 1441. To encourage the negotiation of an acceptable international treaty, no commercial recovery may commence under the Act until 1988 (but exploration and other preliminary activities may commence sooner). 30 U.S.C. § 1412(c). The Act acknowledges United States support of the Declaration of Principles, but states its legal opinion that the exploration and exploitation of the deep seabed is a freedom of the high seas, subject to a duty of reasonable regard to the rights and interests of other states. 30 U.S.C. § 1401.

Several other industrialized nations (the Federal Republic of Germany, Great Britain, France, the Soviet Union and Japan) followed the lead of the United States and passed "interim" national legislation regulating the exploration and exploitation of deep seabed mineral resources. See respectively 20 I.L.M. 393 (1981), as amended, 21 id. 832 (1982); 20 id. 1217 (1981); 21 id. 808 (1982); 21 id. 551 (1982); 22 id. 102 (1983). The developing states have opposed these laws as illegal under international law. See the legal position of the Group of 77, U.N. Doc. A/CONF.62/106 (1980), 14 UNCLOS III, Off. Rec. 111 (1982). For a general comparison of these national acts, see Luoma, "A Comparative Study of National Legislation Concerning the

Deep Sea Mining of Manganese Nodules," 14 J. Maritime L. & Com. 243 (1983).

In 1982, UNCLOS III approved the LOS Convention by 130 votes to 4 (Israel, Turkey, United States, and Venezuela), with 17 abstentions. The United States refused to sign the LOS Convention on the basis that the deep seabed mining regime provisions of the LOS Convention were "hopelessly flawed." White House Office of Policy Information, The Law of the Sea Convention, Issue Update No. 10 (April 15, 1983), at 8. The United States explained that it considered this text unacceptable because it: would actually deter future development of deep seabed mineral resources (because of lack of certainty with regard to the granting of mining contracts, the artificial limitations on seabed mineral production, and the imposition of burdensome financial requirements); would not give the United States an adequate role in the decision-making process; would allow amendments to the Convention to enter into force for the United States without its approval; would provide for mandatory transfer of private technology related to seabed mining; and would allow the transfer of a portion of funds received from the miners by the International Seabed Authority to national liberation movements. "Law of the Sea and Oceans Policy: Statements by President Reagan and Ambassador Malone" on July 9 and August 12, 1982, respectively, U.S. Department of State, Current Policy No. 416 (1982).

The rejection by the United States of the LOS Convention raises the issue of whether the Convention may become binding upon the United States. Since the beginning of the UNCLOS III negotiations, the United States has asserted that it would never be bound by an international deep seabed regime established by a treaty to which it did not consent, and it reserved its right to mine the deep seabed in the absence of an acceptable regime. For a statement of the United States position, see 9 UNCLOS III, Off. Rec. 104 (1976). The Declaration of Principles provides that a deep seabed mining regime shall be established by "an international treaty of a universal character, generally agreed upon." 25 U.N. G.A.O.R., Supp. No. 28, at 24, U.N. Doc. A/8028 (1970). The meaning of "generally agreed upon" is not clear, but would seem to require a very broad consensus. As of 1983, only nine states have ratified the LOS Convention, none of which are the developed states which currently have the technology to mine the deep seabed. If a number of important states should oppose the regime established by the Convention, it would not be "generally agreed upon." However, in the event that a preponderant majority of all regional groups, and of both the developed and developing states, accept the regime established by the Convention and conform their practice to the regime, and the practice is acquiesced in as well by non-parties to the Convention, it may crystallize into customary international law binding upon non-parties.

## B.  SEABED MINING UNDER THE LOS CONVENTION

Under the LOS Convention, the mineral resources of the seabed are the common heritage of mankind and may be exploited only in accordance with the Convention.  LOS Convention, Articles 136 and 137.  No state may claim, exercise sovereign rights over or appropriate any part of the deep seabed or its resources.  Id., Article 137(1).

The Convention establishes an Authority, which shall act on behalf of mankind in governing the deep seabed.  Id., Articles 137(2), 153 and 156–57.  All states which are parties to the LOS Convention are members of the Authority. Id., Article 156(2).  The Authority consists of an Assembly, a Council and a Secretariat.  Id., Article 158.

The Assembly consists of one representative from each member of the Authority.  Id., Article 159(1).  The Assembly is the "supreme organ" of the Authority and is responsible for establishing general policies.  Id., Article 160(1).

The Council consists of 36 members of the Authority, who are elected on a basis intended to assure representation of consumers of minerals to be produced by deep seabed mining, investors in deep seabed mining activities, terrestrial producers of the same minerals, developing states, and a balanced geographical distribution of the members. Id., Article 161. The Council is the "executive organ" of the Authority, with responsibility to establish "specific policies" and to approve "plans of work" for each mining project. Id., Article 162.

The "Enterprise" is the separate legal entity which will carry out mining activities on behalf of the Authority, either directly or through joint ventures with national or private companies. Id., Article 170.

Annex III to the LOS Convention sets forth the basic conditions of exploring and exploiting the deep seabed. Only those applicants who are controlled by states parties to the LOS Convention or by their citizens may apply for a license to explore and exploit the deep seabed. Id., Article 153. The applicant must submit a "plan of work" which describes the intended activity and the site in which it will occur. In its plan, the applicant must present two sites of estimated equal commercial value. If the plan is approved, the Authority reserves one of the sites for the Enterprise, and the applicant acquires exploration and exploitation rights in the other. Under this "parallel system," the Enterprise may relinquish its reserved site to a developing country. Id., Annex III, Articles 8 and 9.

The applicant must disclose to the Authority information relating to the equipment and methods to be used under the plan of work and other non-proprietary technology. Id., Annex III, Article 5(1). Upon approval of a plan, the contractor must make available to the Enterprise (or to a developing country exploiting the reserved site) the technology to be used in the project to the extent the applicant is authorized to transfer the technology, upon fair and reasonable terms, if the technology is not reasonably available in the open market. Id., Annex III, Article 5(3). Any disputes arising from the determination of "fair and reasonable" terms shall be resolved by commercial arbitration. Id., Annex III, Article 5(4). The duty to transfer technology will not apply to contracts concluded ten years after the Enterprise begins commercial production. Id., Annex III, Article 5(7). Where the technology is owned by a third person, the contractor must undertake to obtain approval to transfer this technology, or he himself may not use it. Id., Annex III, Article 5(3)(b).

In consideration of a permit to explore for and exploit the resources of the deep seabed, the contractor must make payments to the Authority. Contractors must pay a one-time fee for the processing of the application in the amount of $500,000. Id., Annex III, Article 13(2). In the event the permit is granted, a contractor must pay an annual fixed fee of $1 million until the date of commencement of commercial production. Id., Annex III, Article 13(3). Thereafter, the contractor shall pay the greater of $1 million or the "production charge." Id. A contractor may choose between two methods of determining the "production charge." Id., Annex III, Article 13(4). Under the first method, the contractor pays a fixed production charge of 5 percent of the market value of the processed metals during the first ten years of commercial production, and at a rate of 12 percent of the market value thereafter. Id., Annex III, Article 13(5). Under the second method the contractor pays a fixed fee of 2 percent of the market value of the processed metals during the first period of commercial production, which rises to 4 percent in the second period of production. Id., Annex III, Article 13(6). In addition, the contractor pays a share of its net proceeds to the Authority after it has recovered its development costs on a graduated scale of 35 to 70 percent. Id., Annex III, Article 13(6)(c).

Since the Enterprise may not have sufficient funds upon its formation to begin exploitation of a reserved site, states parties to the LOS Convention shall make available to it the necessary funds for commercial exploitation of an initial site, in accordance with the scale of assessments for the United Nations general budget. Such funds would be partially in the form of long-term interest-free loans, and partially in the form of guarantees. Id., Annex IV, Article 11(3).

In order to protect the economies of developing countries which currently mine the minerals contained in deep seabed manganese nodules, the Authority is entitled to establish, during an interim 25-year period and within certain strict limits, production quotas for seabed mining. Id., Article 151(2). The Authority is also authorized to participate in commodity conferences and agreements (id., Article 151(1)(b)), and to take compensatory and economic assistance measures for the benefit of developing country producers (id., Article 151(10)).

The LOS Convention establishes as a part of the International Tribunal for the Law of the Sea (see Chapter XII) a Seabed Disputes Chamber which has jurisdiction over disputes between states parties concerning the interpretation or application of the deep seabed regime of the Convention. For example, the Chamber has jurisdiction over: disputes between a state party and the Authority; disputes between parties to a contract and the Authority or the Enterprise concerning the interpretation or application of a contract or plan of work; and disputes between the Authority and an applicant concerning the denial of a contract. Id., Article 187.

For a detailed presentation of the LOS Convention deep seabed mining regime, see W. Hauser, The Legal Regime for Deep Seabed Mining Under the Law of the Sea Convention (Dielmann trans. 1983).

## C. UNITED STATES LEGISLATION

The 1980 Deep Seabed Hard Mineral Resources Act (see Section A, supra) establishes an interim program to regulate the exploration for and commercial recovery of hard mineral resources of the deep seabed by United States citizens. 30 U.S.C. §§ 1401 et seq.

The Act prohibits United States citizens from engaging in the exploration or commercial recovery of deep seabed mineral resources unless authorized to do so under the Act. 30 U.S.C. § 1411 (a). "United States citizen" is defined as any individual citizen; any corporation or other legal entity organized under any United States laws; and any corporation or other entity organized under the laws of a foreign nation if the controlling interest of such entity is held by a United States citizen or entity. 30 U.S.C. § 1403(14). This provision precludes United States citizens from engaging in deep seabed mining activities under the laws of another nation. In addition, those permitted to engage in commercial exploitation of deep seabed minerals under the Act must use United States vessels for processing at sea and at least one United States vessel for transportation services. If processing occurs on land, it must occur in the United States unless otherwise allowed after an agency hearing. 30 U.S.C. § 1412(2), (3), and (5).

The Act establishes a "license" for exploration and a "permit" for commercial recovery of deep seabed mineral resources. A valid existing license entitles an otherwise eligible holder to a permit for commercial recovery. 30 U.S.C. § 1412 (b)(3). As "permits" for commercial recovery may not be issued which authorize production to commence before January 1, 1988 (30 U.S.C. § 1412(c)(1)(D)), regulations governing the issuance of permits have not yet been issued.

To qualify for a license to explore for deep seabed mineral resources, an applicant must be certified by the Administrator of the National Oceanic and Atmospheric Administration (NOAA) as financially responsible and technologically capable of carrying out the exploration and commercial recovery proposed to be undertaken by the applicant. 30 U.S.C. § 1413(c). Applicants must submit an exploration plan which presents the activities to be undertaken, a description of the area to be explored, an exploration schedule, a description of the exploration methods to be used, a description of the recovery and processing technology expected to be used in the recovery state, an estimated schedule of expenditures, and measures to protect the environment. 15 C.F.R. § 970.203. The NOAA Administrator will not accept an application or issue a license for an exploration area larger than 150,000 square kilometers. 15 C.F.R. § 970.601. Upon application, the applicant must submit a $100,000 fee to cover license application review costs. 15 C.F.R. § 970.-208.

After receipt of an application, the NOAA Administrator must consult with other federal agencies, must draft an environmental impact statement and must hold public hearings on the application. 15 C.F.R. §§ 970.211–.212. Procedures are set forth to resolve any conflicts between United States citizens or between a United States citizen and a citizen of a reciprocating state where claims overlap. 15 C.F.R. § 970.302.

Before a license or permit may be issued, the Administrator must find in writing that a proposed exploration or recovery plan will not unreasonably interfere with the exercise of the freedoms of the high seas by other states, will not conflict with any international obligations of the United States, will not create a situation which may lead to a breach of international peace leading to armed conflict, will not adversely affect the environment, and will not endanger safety of life at sea. 30 U.S.C. § 1415(a).

An exploration license shall last for a period of ten years, unless earlier revoked. The license may be renewed for subsequent periods of not more than five years each. 15 C.F.R. § 970.515. As a condition of the license, the licensee must comply with the terms of each exploration license and must diligently pursue exploration. 15 C.F.R. § 970.517. The licensee must comply with the environmental protection measures provided for in the license (15 C.F.R. §§ 970.518, 970.700–.702), and he must ensure that the exploration activities do not unreasonably interfere with the rights of others to exercise the freedoms of the high seas (15 C.F.R. § 970.520).

Permits for commercial recovery of deep seabed minerals will be issued under forthcoming regulations for a period of at least twenty years, unless terminated earlier by reason of insufficient commercial production. 30 U.S.C. § 1417(b).

Applicants who have begun exploring prior to the establishment of the 1980 Act receive priority in the issuance of licenses. 15 C.F.R. §§ 970.300 et seq.

A license or permit issued under the Act authorizes the holder thereof to engage in exploration or commercial recovery to the exclusion of any other United States citizen or any citizen or entity organized under the laws of a "reciprocating state." 30 U.S.C. § 1412(b)(2). A "reciprocating state" is a nation which has enacted similar interim legislation regulating the exploration for and commercial recovery of deep seabed mineral resources which recognizes licenses and permits issued under the United States Act. 30 U.S.C. § 1428. See the 1982 Agreement concerning Interim Arrangements relating to Polymetallic Nodules of the Deep Sea Bed (France, Federal Republic of Germany, United Kingdom, United States) which provides for resolution of overlapping claims of explorers who have engaged in exploration prior to the enactment of relevant national legislation. 21 I.L.M. 950 (1982).

In the event that an international deep seabed treaty does enter into force with respect to the United States, licenses and permits issued under the Act are subject to termination. However, it is the intent of Congress that any future treaty be negotiated in such a way as to provide security of tenure for licensees and permittees under the Act. 30 U.S.C. § 1442.

The Act establishes a Deep Seabed Revenue Sharing Trust Fund. 30 U.S.C. § 1472. The Internal Revenue Code imposes a tax on the removal of hard mineral resources from the deep seabed in the amount of 3.75 percent of the "imputed" value of the resource. 26 U.S.C. § 4495 (b). "Imputed" value is defined as 20 percent of the fair market value of the commercially recovered metals and minerals, which amounts to an overall tax rate of .75 percent of the fair market value of the metals after processing. 26 U.S.C. § 4497. If an international deep seabed treaty is in effect with respect to the United States on or before June 28, 1990, amounts in the Trust Fund shall be available for making contributions required under such treaty. If a treaty is not in effect by that date, amounts in the Trust Fund shall be available for such purposes as Congress may provide.  30 U.S.C. § 1472(d) and (e).

# CHAPTER X

## PROTECTION AND PRESERVATION OF THE MARINE ENVIRONMENT

### A. GENERAL PRINCIPLES

Prior to several marine environmental disasters in the 1960's, such as the Torrey Canyon catastrophe of 1967 in which approximately 120,000 tons of oil were spilled, polluting over 250 miles of coastline of the United Kingdom and France, there were few international conventions for the preservation of the marine environment and its protection against pollution. Several nations had enacted unilateral legislation prohibiting the pollution of their internal waters and their territorial seas, but these acts were inadequate to prevent pollution of waters beyond zones of national jurisdiction and they dealt primarily with pollution caused by the deliberate or grossly negligent discharge of oil from vessels. See, for instance, the Oil Pollution Act of 1924, 43 Stat. 604 (amended by 80 Stat. 1246 (1966), repealed by 86 Stat. 816 (1972)).

At the First United Nations Conference on the Law of the Sea, a comprehensive regime relating to the prevention of pollution and the preservation of the marine environment was not addressed, but some general provisions relating to the obligations of states in this regard were adopted. Article 24 of the 1958 Convention on the High Seas imposes a general obligation on states to regulate the discharge of oil from ships or pipelines or resulting from the exploration or exploitation of the seabed and its subsoil. Article 25 requires states to take measures to prevent pollution of the seas from the dumping of radioactive waste, and it requires states to cooperate with the appropriate international organizations in taking measures for the prevention of pollution of the seas resulting from any activities with radioactive materials or other harmful agents. Article 5(7) of the 1958 Convention on the Continental Shelf requires coastal states to undertake, in safety zones around artificial installations, all appropriate measures for the protection of the living resources of the sea from harmful agents.

The marine disasters of the 1960's fostered the growing recognition that cooperative international action was necessary to protect adequately the marine environment. In 1972 in Stockholm, the United Nations Conference on the Human Environment adopted a Declaration establishing principles and guidelines for government action. For an analysis of the Declaration, see Sohn, "The Stockholm Declaration on the Human Environment," 14 Harv. Int'l L.J. 423 (1973). Principle 7 of the Declaration adopted by the Conference provides that "[s]tates shall take all possible steps to prevent pollution of the seas." Principle 21 provides that states must ensure, in exercising their sovereign rights to exploit their resources, "that activities within their jurisdiction or control do not cause damage to the environment of other States or of areas beyond the limits of national jurisdiction." U.N. Doc. A/CONF. 48/14/Rev. 1, U.N. Pub. E.73.II.A.14, at 3, 4–5 (1972). The latter principle is derived from the seminal Trail Smelter Case, in which the United States and Canada submitted to an international arbitral tribunal a dispute involving injuries caused in the state of Washington by large amounts of sulphur dioxide emitted by a smelter plant in Trail, British Columbia. The Tribunal declared as a principle of international law that "no state has the right to use or permit the use of its territory in such a manner as to cause injury by fumes in or to the territory of another or the properties or persons therein, when the case is of serious consequence and the injury is established by clear and convincing evidence." 3 U.N.R.I.A.A. 1938, 1965 (1941). See, Read, "The Trail Smelter Dispute," 1 Can.Y.B. Int'l L. 213 (1963).

In the 1960's and 1970's, several regional and multilateral conventions emerged governing various aspects of the marine environment. The principles and standards incorporated in the Declaration and in these various conventions served as a basis for the negotiation of a comprehensive regime for the protection and preservation of the marine environment at the Third United Nations Conference on the Law of the Sea. Article 192 of the LOS Convention sets forth the general obligation of states to protect and preserve the marine environment. To fulfill this obligation, states are required to take, individually or jointly, all measures necessary to prevent pollution of the marine environment from any source, using the best practicable means at their disposal and in accordance with their capabilities. LOS Convention, Article 194(1). These measures must take into account internationally agreed rules and standards, and, in some circumstances, must be not less effective than generally accepted international rules and standards. See id., Articles 207(1), 208(3), 209(2), 210(6), and 211(2). The measures taken must encompass all sources of pollution of the marine environment, including:

(1) The release of toxic, harmful or noxious substances from land-based sources, from or through the atmosphere, or by dumping;

(2) Pollution from vessels;

(3) Pollution from installations and devices used in the exploration or exploitation of the natural resources of the seabed and

[*194*]

subsoil and from other installations operating in the marine environment.
Id., Article 194(3). In taking measures to prevent marine pollution, states may not transfer, directly or indirectly, damage or hazards from one area to another or transfer one type of pollution into another. Id., Article 195.

Article 197 of the LOS Convention requires states to cooperate on a regional and global basis, directly or through competent international organizations, in formulating international rules and standards for the protection of the marine environment. A source of controversy throughout the LOS Conference was whether standards should be established on a global or regional basis. See Kindt, "The Effect of Claims by Developing Countries on LOS International Marine Pollution Negotiations," 20 Va. J. Int'l L. 313, 328–32 (1980). To achieve consensus several parallel provisions were adopted. With regard to pollution from land-based sources and from seabed activities within zones of national jurisdiction, states are required to harmonize their policies at a regional level. LOS Convention, Articles 207(3) and 208(4). With regard to pollution from land-based sources, seabed activities subject to national jurisdiction, pollution by dumping, and pollution of the marine environment through or from the atmosphere, states shall endeavor to establish global and regional rules

[*195*]

and standards, acting especially through competent international organizations or diplomatic conferences. Id., Articles 207(4), 208(5), 210(4) and 212(3). With regard to control of pollution from land-based sources, the economic capacity of developing states and their need for economic development must be considered in establishing such standards. Id., Article 207(4).

With regard to deep seabed mining activities, international rules, regulations and procedures are to be adopted by the International Sea-Bed Authority. Id., Articles 145 and 209. See also id., Articles 162(2)(w) and 165(2)(d), (e) and (k).

## B.   VESSEL SOURCE POLLUTION

Article 211 of the LOS Convention requires states, acting through the competent international organization (primarily the International Maritime Organization (IMO, formerly IMCO)) or general diplomatic conference (such as the Brussels Conferences), to establish international rules and standards governing vessel-source pollution, including the adoption of routing systems designed to avoid collisions at sea. Under the Convention, differing types of regulatory jurisdiction are accorded to flag states, and to coastal states with respect to vessels within their ports, within their territorial sea, and within their exclusive economic zone. Article 211(3)–(6).

## 1. Flag State Jurisdiction

Flag states are obligated to adopt laws and regulations for the prevention of pollution of the marine environment from vessels flying their flag or of their registry, which measures must be at least as effective as generally accepted international standards. In particular, flag states must regulate the design, construction, equipment, operation and manning of vessels; and they must take measures for preventing accidents (including the designation of routing systems), dealing with emergencies, ensuring the safety of operations at sea, and preventing both intentional and unintentional discharges. Id., Articles 194(3)(b) and 211. The flag state has the primary responsibility for ensuring that its ships comply with international rules and standards and those of the flag state. Id., Article 217 (see Section I infra).

In exercising its flag state authority, the United States imposes upon United States vessels stringent standards for the design, construction, operation and manning of vessels which are intended to protect the marine environment. See, e.g., 46 U.S.C. § 391a and regulations at 33 C.F.R. Part 157, 46 C.F.R. Part 306 (relating to United States vessels carrying cargoes of hazardous materials in bulk). See also 33 U.S.C. §§ 1001 et seq., implementing the 1954 Oil Pollution Prevention Convention which will be superseded by the 1980 Act to Prevent Pollution from Ships, 33 U.S.C. §§

[*197*]

1901 et seq. upon the entrance into force of the 1978 Protocol to the 1978 International Convention for the Prevention of Pollution from Ships "MARPOL Protocol"), and accompanying regulations at 33 C.F.R. Part 151. The United States is a party to the 1972 Convention on Preventing Collisions at Sea, and it has enacted regulations with which all United States vessels (and foreign vessels passing through waters subject to United States jurisdiction) must comply. 33 U.S.C. §§ 1602, 1603 and 1604.

2. *Coastal State Jurisdiction in Ports and in the Territorial Sea*

Coastal states may adopt laws and regulations for the prevention, reduction and control of marine pollution from foreign vessels within their territorial sea, including vessels exercising the right of innocent passage. However, such measures may not impede innocent passage. LOS Convention, Article 211(4). States may establish standards for pollution prevention as a condition for entrance into their ports or internal waters or for a call at their off-shore terminals (see Chapter V, Section B) but must publicize such requirements, both directly and through the competent international organization. When a port state has harmonized its port entrance policies with other states in the region, a flag state shall require its vessels destined to a port in such region to furnish certain information relating to their compliance with port entry requirements when requested by any cooperating state through the territorial sea of which it is passing. Id., Article 211(3).

In exercising these rights, the United States prohibits the discharge of oil or hazardous substances in its territorial sea. 33 U.S.C. § 1321(b) (3). For a list of hazardous substances subject to this provision, see 40 C.F.R. § 116.4. Vessels within the territorial sea, including foreign vessels exercising their right of innocent passage, may not discharge there any untreated sewage. 33 U.S.C. § 1322; 33 C.F.R. Part 159.

The 1978 Port and Tanker Safety Act conditions port entrance of tankers and other vessels carrying bulk cargoes upon fulfilling specified requirements aimed at minimizing risks to the marine environment. 33 U.S.C. § 1228; 33 C.F.R. Part 157, 46 C.F.R. Part 30. The Act also authorizes the establishment of port access routes designed to prevent collisions. 33 U.S.C. § 1223 (c). These requirements do not apply to foreign vessels exercising their right of innocent passage. 33 U.S.C. § 1223(d).

## 3. Coastal State Jurisdiction in the EEZ

Where a coastal state believes that international rules and standards are inadequate to protect an area of its EEZ, the coastal state may submit a request to the competent international organization for a determination that special conditions exist which merit additional coastal state regulation of vessel-source pollution in that area. Upon a finding that special conditions exist, the coastal state may adopt laws and regulations for the area, which may relate to discharges or navigational practices, but which may not relate to design, construction, manning or equipment standards, other than generally accepted international standards. Id., Article 211(6). See also Section H, infra.

The United States prohibits discharge of oil or hazardous substances within its EEZ, except where permitted under the 1954 Convention (or the MARPOL Protocol, upon its entrance into force.) 33 U.S.C. § 1321(b)(3). In addition, regulations enacted to implement the 1978 MARPOL Protocol, 33 U.S.C. §§ 1901 et seq., and the 1972 Convention on Preventing Collisions at Sea, 33 U.S.C. §§ 1601 et seq., apply to foreign vessels within the United States EEZ.

## C.  POLLUTION FROM LAND–BASED SOURCES

All states, whether coastal or land-locked, must take measures, including the adoption of laws and regulations, to prevent pollution of the marine environment from land-based sources, including rivers, estuaries, pipelines, and outfall structures, taking into account global or regional rules and standards. LOS Convention, Article 207. Lower standards may be established for developing country regions (see Section A, supra).

Several regional agreements regarding pollution from land-based sources have been adopted. See, e.g., the 1980 Protocol for the Protection of the Mediterranean Sea Against Pollution from Land-Based Sources; the 1974 Paris Convention for the Prevention of Marine Pollution from Land-Based Sources (relating to the North Atlantic and Arctic Oceans); and the 1974 Helsinki Convention on the Protection of the Marine Environment of the Baltic Sea.  In several of these conventions, two categories of pollutants are identified: "hazardous" substances and "noxious" substances.  Generally, the introduction of hazardous substances into the sea is to be eliminated. The introduction of noxious substances into the sea is to be strictly controlled, and generally may be done in significant quantities only after the issuance of a permit by designated authorities. Each of the conventions establishes a regional commission to administer the convention.  See Boczek, "International Protection of the Baltic Sea Environment Against Pollution: A Study in Marine Regionalism," 72 A.J.I.L. 782 (1978).

The discharge of pollutants from land-based sources into navigable waters of the United States is strictly regulated under the 1972 Clean Water Act, as amended, 33 U.S.C. §§ 1251 et seq.  The discharge of any pollutant into the navigable waters of the United States (including the territorial sea and adjacent waters) is prohibited unless a permit is issued in compliance with the Act. 33 U.S.C. § 1311. Permits may not be issued for high-level radioactive wastes and for other designated toxic pollutants. 33 U.S.C. §§ 1311(f) and 1317(a). Permits for the discharge of other pollutants shall be issued only if such discharge meets effluent limitations at the source of the discharge and does not violate ambient water quality standards. 33 U.S.C. §§ 1311 and 1313.

## D. OCEAN DUMPING

States are required to adopt laws and regulations to prevent pollution of the marine environment by the dumping of sewage, sludge, and other waste materials into the ocean. See LOS Convention, Article 1(5). These laws and regulations must be no less effective than global rules and standards. States must ensure that dumping is not carried out without the permission of the proper authorities of the state involved. Dumping within the territorial sea and the exclusive economic zone or onto the continental shelf may not occur without the express prior approval of the coastal state, which has the right to permit, regulate and control such dumping. Id., Article 210.

The 1972 Convention on the Dumping of Wastes at Sea, to which the United States is a party, sets forth three categories of waste materials. Parties to the Convention agree to prohibit dumping of materials listed in Annex I, including high-level radioactive wastes, materials produced for biological and chemical warfare, non-biodegradable synthetic materials, petroleum products, and certain toxic compounds. Other categories of waste materials, such as low-level radioactive wastes, require a special prior permit, and a third category of waste materials requires only a general prior permit. Annex III lists terms and conditions upon which general and special permits should be issued. See Duncan, "The 1972 Convention on the Prevention of Marine Pollution by Dumping of Wastes at Sea," 5 J. Mar. L. & Com. 299 (1974).

The 1972 Marine Protection, Research and Sanctuaries Act, as amended, makes unlawful the dumping of material by United States vessels into the territorial sea and waters beyond it and by foreign vessels in the United States territorial sea or contiguous zone unless in compliance with the Act. 33 U.S.C. § 1411. The Secretary of the Army is authorized to issue permits for dredged materials, 33 U.S.C. § 1413, and the Administrator of the Environmental Protection Agency ("EPA") has permit authority for all other wastes, 33 U.S.C. § 1412. Original prohibitions concerning permits for high-level radioactive wastes and chemical and biological warfare agents were modified in 1974 and 1983. See 33 U.S.C. §§ 1411(a) and 1414(h) and (i). After notice and opportunity for public hearing, the Administrator may issue permits for ocean dumping upon determining that such dumping will not "unreasonably degrade or endanger human health, welfare, or amenities, or the marine environment, ecological systems, or economic potentialities." 33 U.S.C. § 1412(a). In making his determination, the Administrator must take into consideration designated factors, including: the need for the proposed dumping; the effect of the dumping on human health and welfare, fisheries resources, shorelines, and marine ecosystems; and the use of land-based alternatives. Id. Permits for the dumping of sewage sludge (a common practice among coastal cities) was to be prohibited after 1981, as well as most permits for the dumping of industrial waste. Id. However, the 1981 deadline has been interpreted by one court to require the denial of permits only for dumping which the EPA determines will unreasonably degrade the environment, taking into account the designated factors mentioned above. City of New York v. Environmental Protection Agency, 543 F.Supp. 1084, 1115 (S.D.N.Y.1981) (EPA may not refuse to issue permit for ocean dumping of sewage sludge to New York City without evaluating the

environmental effects of land disposal). See
Spirer, "The Ocean Dumping Deadline: Easing
the Mandate Millstone," 11 Fordham Urban L.J.
1 (1982). For a list of approved ocean dumping
sites pending completion of environmental studies,
see 40 C.F.R. § 228.12. For a discussion of ocean
dumping of radioactive wastes, see Finn, "Ocean
Disposal of Radioactive Wastes: The Obligation
of International Cooperation to Protect the Marine Environment," 21 Va.J. Int'l L. 621 (1981).

### E. POLLUTION FROM SEABED ACTIVITIES SUBJECT TO NATIONAL JURISDICTION

States are obligated to adopt laws, regulations
and other measures to prevent pollution of the
marine environment arising from or in connection
with their exploration and exploitation of the
seabed and subsoil, or from artificial islands,
installations and structures under their jurisdiction. Such laws, regulations, and measures must
be no less effective than international standards.
LOS Convention, Articles 194(3)(c) and 208.

Under the Outer Continental Shelf Lands Act,
environmental studies must be conducted by the
Secretary of the Interior in all regions in which
oil and gas leases will be sold. 43 U.S.C. § 1346.
Scheduled oil and gas lease sale programs must
achieve a proper balance between environmental,
economic and coastal state concerns. 43 U.S.C.

§ 1344; California v. Watt, 668 F.2d 1290 (D.C. Cir. 1981) (proposed program failed to take into consideration relevant environmental factors). Plans for the production of oil and gas submitted by lessees must provide environmental safeguards. 43 U.S.C. § 1351(c). Environmental impact statements must be prepared by the Secretary of the Interior for a production plan submitted by a lessee. The Secretary shall disappove any plan which may cause serious harm or damage to the marine environment. 43 U.S.C. §§ 1351(e)–(h). It is the duty of any lessee to maintain all operations within the lease area in compliance with environmental protection regulations. 43 U.S.C. § 1348(b). For a discussion of liability for environmental damage arising from continental shelf mining activities, see Section I.

Licenses for the construction and operation of deepwater ports may not be issued until an environmental impact statement has been prepared and reviewed. 33 U.S.C. §§ 1504(f) and 1505. Regulations have been issued to prevent pollution of the marine environment, to clean up any pollutants which may be discharged, and to minimize any adverse environmental impact from the construction and operation of deepwater ports. 33 C.F.R. Parts 149 and 150.

## F. POLLUTION FROM DEEP
## SEABED MINING

For states parties to the LOS Convention, international rules, regulations and procedures to prevent pollution of the marine environment from deep seabed activities shall be issued in accordance with Part XI of the Convention. Article 145 of Part XI authorizes the Authority to adopt appropriate rules and regulations (see Chapter X, Section A, supra).

The 1980 Deep Seabed Hard Mineral Resources Act incorporates extensive rules relating to the protection of the marine environment against pollution which might result from deep seabed activities carried on by persons subject to United States jurisdiction. The Administrator of the National Oceanic and Atmospheric Administration is required to conduct a deep ocean mining environmental study and to conduct ongoing related research programs. 30 U.S.C. § 1419(a). Each license and permit issued under the Act must contain provisions for safeguarding the environment. 30 U.S.C. § 1419(b). Licenses and permits may be issued only after preparation and approval of an environmental impact study. 30 U.S.C. § 1419(d). The discharge of pollutants from any vessel engaged in exploration or commercial recovery of deep seabed mineral resources is subject to the Clean Water Act (33 U.S.C. §§ 1251 et seq.). 30 U.S.C. § 1419(e).

Each licensee or permittee is required to monitor the environmental effects of any deep seabed exploration and mining activities and to submit relevant information to the Administrator. 30 U.S.C. § 1424. For a discussion of liability for pollution arising from deep seabed activities, see Section I, infra.

## G. POLLUTION FROM OR THROUGH THE ATMOSPHERE

All states are required to adopt laws, regulations and measures to prevent pollution of the marine environment from or through the atmosphere. These rules and regulations shall govern activities within air space under their sovereignty, and must be observed by vessels flying their flag or aircraft under their registry. Such rules and regulations shall take into account international rules and standards.

More than 100 states have become parties to the 1963 Limited Test Ban Treaty. States parties are bound not to conduct the testing of nuclear weapons anywhere but underground, and not even there if radioactive debris would travel outside the testing state's territory.

## H. PROTECTION OF FRAGILE ECOSYSTEMS

States are obligated to take measures necessary to protect and preserve rare or fragile ecosystems as well as the habitat of depleted, threatened or endangered species and other forms of marine life. Where the area to be protected forms part of a state's exclusive economic zone, special international arrangements must be made to prevent the pollution of such a zone. LOS Convention, Articles 194(5) and 211(6).

A coastal state also has the right to adopt and enforce non-discriminatory laws and regulations for the prevention, reduction and control of marine pollution from vessels in ice-covered areas within the limits of its exclusive economic zone, where particularly severe climatic conditions and the presence of ice for most of the year create obstructions or exceptional hazards to navigation. Such laws and regulations are needed especially where pollution of the marine environment could cause major harm to, or irreversible disturbance of, the ecological balance. Id., Article 234.

These principles reflect the consensus developed at the Third United Nations Law of the Sea Conference. Previously, a controversy was caused by the enactment by Canada in 1970 of the Canadian Arctic Waters Pollution Prevention Act, the purpose of which was to preserve "the peculiar ecological balance that now exists in the water, ice and land areas" of the Canadian Arctic. That legislation established and applied to foreign ships safety control zones extending 100 nautical miles from the nearest Canadian land, north of the sixtieth parallel of latitude and including both liquid and frozen waters within that area. All ships not complying with far-reaching Canadian regulations were banned from these zones. 18–19 Eliz. II, c. 47 (1969–70), Can.Rev.Stat. ch. C–2 (1970); 9 I.L.M. 543 (1970). For the United States objections to the Canadian measures and the Canadian response, see 9 I.L.M. 605–15 (1970).

# I.  RESPONSIBILITY AND LIABILITY

A state which fails to fulfill its obligations to protect and preserve the marine environment is liable in accordance with international law. LOS Convention, Article 235(1). Under international law, a state may be required to prevent, reduce or terminate the activity threatening or causing pollution, or to pay reparation for injury caused. See, e.g., The Trail Smelter Case (United States v. Canada), 3 U.N.R.I.A.A. 1911 (1938), 1936 (1941). Where a state's violation of anti-pollution rules or standards results in injury to private interests, the state must ensure that recourse is available in accordance with its legal system for prompt and adequate compensation or other relief. LOS Convention, Article 235(2).

States are obligated to cooperate in developing and implementing international law in order to assure prompt and adequate compensation for damage caused by pollution of the marine environment. These measures may include criteria and procedures for payment of adequate compensation, such as compulsory insurance or compensation funds. Id., Article 235(3).

Several international conventions deal with liability of persons responsible for the violation of international anti-pollution rules or standards. In view of the special concern about nuclear ships, the 1962 Nuclear Ships Convention provides that the operator of a nuclear ship "shall be absolutely liable for any nuclear damage upon proof that such damage has been caused by a nuclear incident involving the nuclear fuel of, or radioactive products or waste produced in, such ship." Id., Article 2. The liability of the operator is limited to 1.5 billion gold francs in respect of any one nuclear incident. Id., Article 3. (For the definition of a gold franc, see id., Article 3(4).) The licensing state, i.e., the state that authorized the operation of a nuclear ship under its flag, is obligated to ensure the payment of claims for compensation for nuclear injury if the insurance or other financial security arranged for by the operator proves to be inadequate. Id., Article 3(2). Claims may be brought, at the option of the claimant, either before the courts of the licensing state or of the state in whose territory nuclear injury has been inflicted. Id., Article 10(1). Any immunity from legal process pursuant to national or international law is to be waived with respect

[*211*]

to obligations arising under this Convention. Id., Article 10(3).  See Könz, "The 1962 Brussels Convention on the Liability of Operators of Nuclear Ships," 57 A.J.I.L. 100 (1963).  As the United States is not a party to this Convention, difficulties arose with respect to admission of the nuclear ship Savannah into foreign ports, and a contingency liability fund was established.  42 U.S.C. § 2210(1).  In addition, the United States was obligated to conclude a series of indemnification agreements with a number of foreign governments that would apply in the event of a nuclear incident.  See 9 Whiteman, Digest of International Law 303–04 (1968).

The 1969 Convention on Civil Liability for Oil Pollution Damage applies exclusively to any injuries caused by oil pollution in the territory, including the territorial sea, of a state party, and provides for compensation for the cost of measures taken to prevent or minimize such injuries. Article 2.  The liability of the owner of the ship that causes oil pollution injuries is limited to 210 million gold francs (id., Article 5(1)), except when the incident occurred as a result of actual fault of, or of someone in privity with, the owner (id., Article 5(2)).  Compensation claims can be brought only in the courts of the state (or one of the states) where the injury occurred, but the judgment of such court is enforceable in any state party to the Convention.  Id., Articles 9(1) and

10(1). (This Convention is not in force for the United States.) A 1976 Protocol modified the limit of liability to "14 million units of account" based on Special Drawing Rights as defined by the International Monetary Fund. Article 2.

As the 1969 Convention did not afford full compensation for victims of oil pollution injuries, but imposed a financial burden on ship owners, a supplementary compensation and indemnification system was established by the 1971 Convention concerning an International Fund for Compensation for Oil Pollution Damage. Contributions to the fund are to be made by persons receiving shipments of oil by sea, in proportion to the tonnage received (Article 10), and any state receiving oil in its territory is obligated to ensure that the contributions are paid (Article 13) and may by special declaration assume the obligation itself (Article 14). A 1976 Protocol revises the financial arrangements provided for by this Convention.

There are also several private international agreements for sharing liability for injuries caused by oil pollution, such as the 1969 Tanker Owners Voluntary Agreement Concerning Liability for Oil Pollution ("TOVALOP") and the 1971 Oil Companies' Contract Regarding an Interim Supplement to Tanker Liability for Oil Pollution ("CRISTAL"). See Becker, "A Short Cruise on the Good Ships TOVALOP and CRISTAL," 5

J.Mar.L. & Com. 609 (1974). There is also a 1974 Offshore Pollution Liability Agreement ("OPOL"), relating to liability for pollution connected with offshore drilling.

Under the Federal Water Pollution Control Act of 1956, as amended, (FWCPA), any owner, operator, or person in charge of a vessel or facility from which oil or a hazardous substance is discharged in harmful quantities into the navigable waters of the United States, its territorial sea, or exclusive economic zone, or in connection with continental shelf exploitation activities or deepwater ports, is subject to a civil penalty of $5,000 for such discharge. 33 U.S.C. § 1321(b)(6)(A). The Administrator of the Environmental Protection Agency may commence an action against such a person to impose further penalties of up to $50,000 ($250,000 in the case of willful negligence or misconduct) taking into account the gravity of the offense and the efforts of the person to mitigate the effects of such discharge. 33 U.S.C. § 1321(b)(6)(B). Failure of a person in charge of a vessel or facility to report a discharge upon its discovery may subject such person to a $10,000 fine and imprisonment of up to one year. 33 U.S.C. § 1321(b)(5).

In addition, such person shall be liable to the United States for the costs of removal of the discharge, unless caused by an act of God or war, negligence on the part of the government, or the act or omission of a third party. 33 U.S.C.

§ 1321(f). For vessels, removal cost liability is limited to the greater of $125 per gross ton or $125,000 for oil barges, and in the case of any other vessel, $150 per gross ton (or $250,000 for vessels carrying oil or a hazardous substance as a cargo), whichever is greater. These limitations do not apply if the discharge is the result of willful negligence or misconduct, in which case costs are recoverable in full. Id. For discharges of a hazardous substance from onshore or offshore facilities, the government may recover up to $50,000 from the responsible person, or all of such costs if the discharge is the result of willful negligence or misconduct. Id.

The government's exclusive remedy for oil spill (as distinguished from hazardous substances) cleanup costs against a discharging vessel or facility are those provided for in the FWCPA. The limits of liability may not be circumvented by allowing the government to pursue other forms of action, such as maritime tort, against the discharger. United States v. Dixie Carriers, Inc., 627 F.2d 736 (5th Cir. 1980). Where a third party (such as a tug boat) is responsible for the discharge, 33 U.S.C. § 1321(g) imposes removal cost liability upon that party, with limitations similar to those of 33 U.S.C. § 1321(f). However, 33 U.S.C. § 1321(h) permits the government or discharger to pursue other remedies against such third party. United States v. M/V Big Sam,

681 F.2d 432 (5th Cir. 1982). Judge Gee, in his dissent from the denial of a petition for a rehearing en banc of the M/V Big Sam case, summarized the disparate treatment of discharging vessels and third party responsible persons as follows: "Thus he who  .  .  .  solely and carelessly causes another to discharge [oil], is to be— in appropriate circumstances—crushed, while he who carried it and carelessly discharged it is to be shielded  .  .  ." Id., 693 F.2d 451, 458 (5th Cir. 1982).

In 1980, the United States Congress enacted the Comprehensive Environmental Response, Compensation, and Liability Act, 42 U.S.C. § 9601 et seq., which establishes a comprehensive regime governing liability for and payment of compensation for damages, including clean-up costs, loss of property, and other damages, caused by the discharge of hazardous substances other than oil or petroleum products into the environment. (The FWCPA continues to govern oil discharges.) The owner or operator of any vessel or facility subject to United States jurisdiction from which there is a release or threatened release of a hazardous substance which causes the incurrence of removal or clean-up costs shall be liable for all costs of removal or remedial action and damages for injury to, destruction of or loss of natural resources (defined in 42 U.S.C. § 9601(16) to include land, fish, wildlife, biota, air, water, and other such resources belonging to the United States, a state, or any foreign government). 42 U.S.C. § 9607(a). The liability of the owner or operator is limited to amounts which vary according to the size and type of vessels and facilities (up to the greater of $5,000,000 or $300 per gross ton for vessels carrying hazardous cargoes). However, liability is unlimited where the discharge is a result of willful misconduct or negligence, where the primary cause of such discharge is a violation of applicable safety, construction, or operation regulations, or where the person responsible fails to provide all reasonable cooperation and assistance to remedial activities. 42 U.S.C. § 9607(c)(2). The only defenses against liability are an act of God, an act of war, or certain acts or omissions of third parties. 42 U.S.C. § 9607(b). Penalties may be imposed for failure to notify the proper government authority immediately of a discharge. 42 U.S.C. § 9603(b). In addition, punitive damages may be assessed where the liable person fails without cause to provide removal or remedial action upon the order of the President. 42 U.S.C. § 9607(c)(3). Unlike the FWCPA, the 1980 Act specifically preserves the rights of the government and others to proceed and recover under other theories of law, so that the limitations of liability under the Act may be overcome. 42 U.S.C. § 9607(j).

The Act establishes a "superfund" to compensate for damages which are not fully compensated by owners and operators. The superfund is funded by excise taxes on owners and operators of vessels and facilities and designated other sources (including trust funds established previously under other acts, such as the 1974 Deepwater Port Act and the 1978 Outer Continental Shelf Land Act Amendments). 42 U.S.C. § 9631. All claims for liability under the Act must first be presented to the owner, operator, or guarantor of the vessel or facility from which oil or a hazardous substance has been released. If the claim has not been satisfied within sixty days, the claimant may present the claim to the superfund or commence an action in court. If the superfund pays the claim, it may commence an action to recover from the owner, operator, or guarantor. 42 U.S.C. § 9612.

For a detailed discussion of the history of the Act, see House Report No. 96–172, reprinted in [1980] U.S. Code Cong. & Adm. News 6160. For a discussion of the overlap and differences between the FWCPA and the Superfund Act, see Helfrich, "Problems in Pollution Response Liability under Federal Laws: FWPCA Section 311 and the Superfund," 13 J.Mar.L. & Com. 455 (1982).

## J. ENFORCEMENT

Jurisdiction to enforce rules and regulations relating to the marine environment can be exercised by flag states, coastal states and port states in varying degrees, depending upon the source of pollution and the location of the violation or the resulting environmental damage.

### 1. *Flag State Enforcement*

The flag state has the primary obligation to ensure that its ships comply with applicable international rules and standards established through the competent international organization or general diplomatic conference, and with the flag state's laws and regulations implementing such standards. LOS Convention, Article 217(1). Flag states may not permit their ships to sail unless they meet such requirements, including standards relating to design, construction, equipment, and manning, as evidenced by certificates of compliance. Id., Article 217(2). Furthermore, flag states must inspect periodically their ships to verify that such certificates are in conformity with the ship's actual condition. Other states must accept these certificates as evidence of the condition of the ship, unless there are clear grounds for believing otherwise. Id., Article 217(3).

If a ship does not meet international rules and standards, the flag state must provide for immediate investigation and, where appropriate, institute proceedings irrespective of where the violation or injury has occurred. Id., Article 217(4). The state that is the victim of a violation by a ship (or, in the case of pollution of the common environment, any state) may complain to the flag state and request it to take appropriate actions (id., Article 217(6)), and, if dissatisfied with the action taken by the flag state, may invoke against the flag state the remedies available under international law (id., Article 235(1)).

Flag states must provide penalties sufficient in severity to discourage violations by their ships whenever they occur. Id., Article 217(8).

In In re Oil Spill by Amoco Cadiz off the Coast of France on March 16, 1978, 699 F.2d 909 (7th Cir. 1983), the court upheld jurisdiction over a claim based upon negligent operation filed by French citizens against various affiliates of Standard Oil Company (Indiana), including Amoco Transport Company, a Liberian company which was the owner of the wrecked vessel. The court reasoned that the true owner of the vessel was the American parent corporation, due to the absence of any significant links between the vessel and the flag state. Id. at 914. In addition, the court upheld jurisdiction of a claim based upon negligent or defective design against the shipbuilder, Astilleros Espanoles, S.H., a Spanish company, and over a cross-claim for indemnification filed by Amoco Transport Company against Astilleros. Id. at 915.

### 2. *Coastal State Enforcement*

The authority of the coastal state to bring proceedings against an offending foreign vessel varies in some respects, depending on where the vessel is located and where the violation occurred. The coastal state has jurisdiction to prescribe, adjudicate and enforce with respect to any matter relating to acts of pollution committed in its ports. In addition, the coastal state can institute proceedings against a ship voluntarily in port or against its crew for a violation of its laws that occurred within its territorial sea or exclusive economic zone, provided that its laws were adopted in accordance with generally accepted rules and standards. An offshore terminal is assimilated for these purposes to a port. LOS Convention, Article 220(1).

Where there are clear grounds for believing that a foreign ship, passing through the territorial sea of the coastal state, has, during that passage, violated laws and regulations of that state adopted in accordance with applicable international rules and standards, the coastal state may, subject to certain procedural safeguards (id., Article 226), undertake physical inspection of the vessel in the territorial sea in order to ascertain the facts relating to the violation. It may, where evidence so warrants, institute proceedings, including detention of the ship, in accordance with its laws. If the act of pollution in the territorial sea was wilful and serious, the coastal state may impose any penalties authorized by its law. Id., Articles 220(2) and 230(2).

When the violation of international anti-pollution rules or standards was committed in the exclusive economic zone of the coastal state, and the ship is still in the exclusive economic zone or the territorial sea of the coastal state, that state can take various steps, depending on the gravity of the violation. Where there are clear grounds for believing that a violation has occurred, the coastal state may require the ship to give information regarding its identity and port of registry, its last and its next port of call, and other relevant information needed to establish whether a violation has occurred. Id., Article 220(3). When, however, there are clear grounds for believing that the violation resulted in "a substantial discharge causing or threatening significant pollution of the marine environment," and the ship either refuses to give information or the information supplied is manifestly in variance with the evident facts, the coastal state is entitled to proceed with a physical inspection. Id., Article 220(5). Only if there is "clear objective evidence" that the ship committed the violation and that the discharge is causing or threatens to cause "major damage to the coastline or related interests of the coastal state, or to any resources of its territorial sea or exclusive economic zone," is that state entitled, if the evidence so warrants, to institute proceedings in accordance with its laws, and to detain the ship. Id., Article 220(6).

To ensure that in no case is a ship unduly detained, appropriate procedures must be established, either through the competent international organization or by special agreement, for bonding or other appropriate financial security. If the ship makes the necessary arrangements, the coastal state is obligated to allow the vessel to proceed. Id., Article 220(7). Monetary penalties only may be applied, unless the violation was committed in the territorial sea and the act of pollution was willful and serious, in which case the vessel may be confiscated and the person responsible may be tried and punished. Id., Article 230.

## 3. *Port State Enforcement*

The jurisdiction of the port state has been enlarged with respect to foreign ships voluntarily in its port or off-shore terminal, to allow the state to investigate and, where the evidence warrants, institute proceedings with respect to any discharge from that ship that occurred on the high seas. Id., Article 218(1). The port state is also entitled to institute proceedings if a discharge violation that occurred outside its coastal waters caused or is likely to cause pollution within those waters. Id., Article 218(2). If the discharge violation occurred in the coastal waters of another state, the port state is obligated to institute proceedings, as far as practicable, when requested by that state. In addition, the port state is obligated to conduct an investigation, as far as practicable, when so requested by the flag state (irrespective of where the violation occurred) or by the state damaged or threatened by the discharge violation. Id., Article 218(3).

The records of the investigation carried out by a port state must be transmitted to the state that asked for the investigation and requested the records. The state in whose coastal waters the violation took place, but not the state where the injury occurred, is entitled to have the proceedings transferred to it. Once the records, the evidence and the bonds (or other financial security) are transmitted to the requesting state, the proceedings in the port state must be suspended. Id., Article 218(4).

*4. Overlapping Jurisdiction*

The flag state is entitled to have penal proceedings against its ship in a foreign state suspended as soon as the flag state has itself instituted proceedings against the ship. There are three exceptions: the state that has instituted the proceedings need not suspend them (1) if the violation was committed in its territorial sea; (2) if the coastal state suffered major damage; or (3) if the flag state "has repeatedly disregarded its obligations to enforce effectively the applicable international rules and standards in respect of violations committed by its vessels." When the proceedings are suspended, they have to be terminated upon completion of proceedings in the flag state. Id., Article 228. If the coastal state is dissatisfied with the action taken by the flag state after the case has been transferred, it may, in accordance with general international law, complain both to the flag state and to the competent international organization; and if the lack of enforcement recurs, the coastal state may next time refuse to suspend proceedings. Id., Article 228(1).

*5. Liability for Wrongful Enforcement*

If a state has taken measures against a foreign ship that were unlawful or exceeded those reasonably required in the light of available information, it is obligated to pay to the flag state appropriate compensation for any injury or loss attributable to such measures. It must also provide for recourse in its legal system for private actions in respect of such injury or loss. Id., Article 232.

Liability for wrongful enforcement measures was provided in the 1958 Convention on the High Seas, though environmental measures are not mentioned there. See Articles 20 (piracy), 22(3) (stopping certain suspected ships on the high seas), and 23(7) (hot pursuit). Article 6 of the 1969 Convention on Intervention on the High Seas provides that any Contracting Party that has taken measures in contravention of the provisions of that convention "shall be obliged to pay compensation to the extent of the damage caused by measures which exceed those reasonably necessary" to prevent, mitigate or eliminate grave and imminent danger. Under the 1973 Convention for the Prevention of Pollution from Ships (MARPOL), a ship that is unduly detained or delayed by measures taken under that convention "shall be entitled to compensation for any loss or damage suffered." Article 7(2).

## K. NOTIFICATION AND COOPERATIVE ACTION

When a state becomes aware that the marine environment has been injured or is in imminent danger of being injured, it has the duty to notify immediately other states likely to be affected by such injuries as well as the competent global or regional international organization. LOS Convention, Article 198.

States in an area affected by a maritime pollution disaster have the duty to cooperate in eliminating the effects of pollution and in preventing or minimizing the injury. To be better able to deal with such emergencies, neighboring states are obligated to develop and be ready to put into operation contingency plans for responding to pollution incidents affecting the marine environment in their vicinity. Id., Article 199. See, for example, 1980 United States-Mexico Marine Pollution Agreement.

## L. GOVERNMENT NONCOMMERCIAL SHIPS

Government noncommercial ships are not subject to the international rules, standards and enforcement procedures discussed above. However, each state must ensure, through the adoption of appropriate measures, that such ships act so far as practicable in a manner consistent with international rules and standards. LOS Convention, Article 236.

# CHAPTER XI

# HIGH SEAS FREEDOM

## A. GENERAL PRINCIPLES

Freedom of the high seas has been a basic precept of the law of the sea since the seventeenth century (see historical comments in the preface, supra). All states, both coastal and land-locked, have the right to exercise the freedom of the high seas. This freedom includes (but is not limited to):

(1) freedom of navigation;

(2) freedom of overflight;

(3) freedom of fishing;

(4) freedom to lay submarine cables and pipelines;

(5) freedom to construct artificial islands, installations and structures; and

(6) freedom of scientific research.

The first four of these freedoms are expressly mentioned in the 1958 Convention on the High Seas (Article 2(11)); the last two were added in Article 87(1) of the LOS Convention. These freedoms must be exercised by all states with reasonable regard to the interests of other states in their exercise of the freedom of the high seas, and states are bound to refrain from any acts which unreasonably interfere with the use of the high seas by nationals of other states. See 1958 Convention on the High Seas, Article 2(2); LOS Convention, Article 87(2) (where "due regard" was substituted for "reasonable regard"). No state may appropriate any part of the high seas or otherwise subject it to that state's sovereignty. 1958 Convention on the High Seas, Article 2(1); LOS Convention, Article 89. All high seas freedoms apply in the waters which do not constitute the internal waters, territorial sea, or exclusive economic zone of a state, or the archipelagic waters of an archipelagic state. LOS Convention, Article 86; see also 1958 Convention on the High Seas, Article 1. The freedoms of navigation and overflight and of laying submarine cables and pipelines and certain associated uses of the sea may be exercised also in the exclusive economic zones of other states, with due regard to the rights and duties of the coastal state, and in compliance with the laws and regulations of the coastal state insofar as they are compatible with international law. LOS Convention, Articles 58 and 86. See Chapter VIII, supra.

## B.  RESERVATION OF THE HIGH SEAS FOR PEACEFUL PURPOSES

The high seas shall be reserved for peaceful purposes. LOS Convention, Article 88. The high seas may be used by naval forces, but their use for aggressive purposes would be in violation of this article and Article 2(4) of the Charter of the United Nations. See also Article 301 of the LOS Convention, which requires states parties in acting under the Convention to refrain from any threat or use of force in violation of the U.N. Charter. For examples of incidents involving the use of force or a threat to use force on the high seas, including the 1962 quarantine of Cuba by United States naval forces, see 4 Whiteman, Digest of International Law 523–42 (1965).

Since 1946, the United States has conducted nuclear weapons tests in the high seas of the Pacific Ocean. The Atomic Energy Commission was authorized to establish danger zones which extended over large portions of the high seas for the tests. United States citizens and other persons under the jurisdiction of the United States were prohibited from entering the danger zones. 42 U.S.C. § 2278a; see, e.g., 23 Fed.Reg. 4782 (establishing a 400-mile radius danger zone). All other vessels were warned to stay clear of the area. The use of the high seas for nuclear tests caused great controversy. See, McDougal & Schlei, "The Hydrogen Bomb Tests in Perspective: Lawful Measures for Security," 64 Yale L.J. 648 (1955); Margolis, "The Hydrogen Bomb Experiments and International Law," 64 Yale L.J. 629 (1955); 4 Whiteman, Digest of International Law 553–607 (1965). In 1963, the Limited Test

Ban Treaty was signed at Moscow. The treaty entered into force for the United States on October 10, 1963, but France and China are not parties to it and continued testing in the atmosphere after 1963. See Nuclear Tests Cases (Australia and New Zealand v. France), 1974 I.C.J. 253, 457.

## C.　FREEDOM OF NAVIGATION

Every state has the right to sail ships flying its flag on the high seas. 1958 Convention on the High Seas, Article 4; LOS Convention, Article 90. However, due consideration for interests of all concerned requires that ships on the high seas observe rules relating to the safety of navigation, the protection of life at sea, and the prevention, reduction and control of pollution of the marine environment. It is primarily the duty of the flag state to regulate its ships in these regards. See Chapter II, Section A, and Chapter X, Section B, infra.

Warships and state-owned or -operated ships, when on the high seas, have complete immunity from jurisdiction of any state other than the flag state. 1958 Convention on the High Seas, Article 8(1) and (9); LOS Convention, Articles 95 and 96. For a definition of "warship," see 1958 Convention on the High Seas, Article 8(2); LOS Convention, Article 29. See Chapter II, Section B.8.

A warship or law enforcement vessel that encounters on the high seas a foreign ship (other than a government noncommercial ship) may board such ship if there is reasonable cause to suspect that it is (1) engaged in piracy, slave trade, traffic in narcotic drugs or unauthorized broadcasting; (2) is without nationality; or (3) is of the same nationality as the warship or law enforcement ship (though flying no flag or a foreign flag). 1958 Convention on the High Seas, Article 22; LOS Convention, Article 110; see Chapter II, supra, relating to rights of enforcement upon the high seas.

Where authorized by international agreement, a warship or law enforcement ship may interfere with the navigation of a foreign ship. See, for instance, Article 2 of the 1953 Canada-United States Northern Pacific Halibut Convention which permits the law enforcement ships of one state party to stop and board ships of the other state party for inspection and, if a violation is found, to seize the ship for delivery to an authorized official of the flag state. Searches conducted under the implementing legislation of the United States (16 U.S.C. § 772d(a)) have been held to be subject to a standard of reasonableness. United States v. Taylor, 488 F.Supp. 475 (D.Ore. 1980). If the suspicions prove to be unfounded, and the boarding was not justified by any act of the ship, international law requires that it be compensated for any loss.   1958 Convention on the High Seas, Article 22(3);  LOS Convention, Article 110(3);  see also Chapter II, supra.

## D.  FREEDOM OF OVERFLIGHT

All civilian and military airplanes have the right to overfly the high seas.  Civil aircraft must observe the Rules of the Air enacted by the International Civil Aviation Organization (ICAO) pursuant to Article 12 of the 1944 Chicago Convention on International Civil Aviation.  State aircraft must operate at all times with due regard for the safety of navigation, and states normally require compliance with safety measures enacted by ICAO.  LOS Convention, Article 39(3) (which relates to transit passage but embodies a general principle).

The United States and other nations have established air defense identification zones which often extend several hundred miles into sea.  See J. Murchisin, The Contiguous Air Space Zone in International Law (1957);  Note, "Air Defense Identification Zone:  Creeping Jurisdiction in the Airspace," 18 Va.J. Int'l L. 485 (1978); 4 Whiteman, Digest of International Law 496–97 (1965).

## E.  FREEDOM OF FISHING

All states have the right to fish on the high seas subject to their treaty obligations and the rights and duties of coastal states (see Chapter VIII, supra).  1958 Fishing on the High Seas

Convention, Article 1; LOS Convention, Article 116. In addition, all states have the duty to take, or to cooperate with other states in taking, such measures as may be necessary for the conservation of the living resources of the high seas, and for the management of the living resources of the high seas, and to ensure that their nationals comply with these measures. States whose nationals exploit identical fisheries or fisheries in the same area must enter negotiations to conserve these resources. States shall, when appropriate, cooperate to establish subregional or regional organizations to this end. 1958 Fishing on the High Seas Convention, Articles 1(2), 2, and 4; LOS Convention, Articles 117 and 118. The United States has entered numerous agreements, bilateral and multilateral, regarding the management and conservation of high seas fisheries. See, for example, the 1953 North Pacific Fisheries Convention (as amended in 1962 and 1978) and implementing legislation at 16 U.S.C. §§ 1021 et seq.

In determining the allowable catch and establishing other conservation measures for high seas fisheries, states must take nondiscriminatory measures designed to maintain and restore species at levels which can produce the maximum sustainable yield, as qualified by relevant environmental and economic factors, taking into account the requirements of developing states, fishing pat-

[234]

terns, the interdependence of stocks, and generally recommended international standards. States must also consider the effects on associated species. LOS Convention, Article 119.

With regard to marine mammals, states must cooperate to conserve them and to work through international organizations for their conservation, management and study. LOS Convention, Articles 65 and 120. See, for example, the 1946 Whaling Convention and United States implementing legislation at 16 U.S.C. §§ 916 et seq. The United States has imposed a moratorium prohibiting United States citizens, vessels, and others within its jurisdiction from taking or importing marine mammals except in limited instances. 16 U.S.C. §§ 1361 et seq.

## F.  FREEDOM TO LAY SUBMARINE CABLES AND PIPELINES

The freedom to lay submarine cables and pipelines is subject to special rules relating to cables and pipelines on the continental shelf. LOS Convention, Articles 79 and 112. Every state must adopt laws and regulations necessary to punish its ships or persons who willfully or through culpable negligence break or injure a submarine cable or pipeline, unless caused with the objective of saving lives or ships. 1958 Convention on the High Seas, Article 27; LOS Convention, Article 113. Every state must adopt laws and regulations

[*235*]

to cause its nationals which own submarine cables or pipelines to bear the costs of repairs incurred if, in laying or repairing cables or pipelines, they injure another cable or pipeline. 1958 Convention on the High Seas, Article 28; LOS Convention, Article 114. Where ships have sacrificed an anchor, net or fishing gear to avoid injury to a cable or pipeline, states must adopt laws and regulations to ensure that the ship owners are indemnified for those costs by the cable or pipeline owner. 1958 Convention on the High Seas, Article 29; LOS Convention, Article 115.

The 1884 Convention for the Protection of Submarine Cables provides for punishment for willful or negligent breaking of or injury to submarine cables outside territorial waters. United States legislation implementing the Act is at 47 U.S.C. §§ 21 et seq. Concerning an incident of alleged damage to United States cables by Soviet vessels (both countries are parties to the 1884 Convention), see 40 Dep't State Bull. 555 (1959).

## G.  FREEDOM TO CONSTRUCT ARTIFICIAL ISLANDS

The freedom to construct artificial islands, installations and structures is subject to special rules relating to constructions on the continental shelf and in the exclusive economic zone. See Chapters VIII and IX. With regard to constructions relating to deep seabed mining activities, see Article 147 of the LOS Convention.

## H. FREEDOM OF SCIENTIFIC RESEARCH

All states as well as competent international organizations have the right to conduct research in the water column beyond the limits of the exclusive economic zone of coastal states. LOS Convention, Article 257. Scientific research in the seabed and subsoil of the continental shelf beyond that limit is, however, restricted to some extent. Id., Article 246(6); see also Chapter VIII, Section E, supra.

In the conduct of marine scientific research the following principles apply:

(1) marine research is to be conducted exclusively for peaceful purposes;

(2) such research may not unjustifiably interfere with other legitimate uses of the sea and in turn is to be duly respected by other users;

(3) such research may not constitute the legal basis for any claim to any part of the marine environment or its resources;

(4) such research may deploy and use any type of scientific research installations or equipment, subject to specified conditions.

LOS Convention, Articles 240–41 and 258–62.

# CHAPTER XII

## SETTLEMENT OF DISPUTES

A state is not bound to go to an international tribunal unless it has accepted previously that tribunal's jurisdiction or agrees by a special agreement (so-called "compromis") to submit a particular dispute to the tribunal. Consequently, when a state has a dispute with another state about an alleged violation of a law of the sea rule, in most cases there is no international tribunal having jurisdiction to decide the issue. If negotiations between the two governments do not lead to a settlement of the dispute, and if the other state cannot be persuaded to submit the dispute to a tribunal by special agreement, then there is no way to resolve the dispute, and it may disturb the relations between the two states for a long time.

To avoid this, many treaties relating to law of the sea problems contain a so-called compromissory clause by which the parties to the treaty agree to submit to an international tribunal any dispute relating to the interpretation or application of that treaty. Several conventions concluded under the auspices of the International Maritime Consultative Organization (now International Maritime Organization) contain provisions authorizing the submission of such disputes to the International Court of Justice or to an arbitral tribunal. See, e.g., 1954 Oil Pollution Prevention Convention, Article 13; 1969 Convention on Intervention on the High Seas, Article 8 and Annex, Articles 13–19. At the 1958 Conference on the Law of the Sea, no agreement could be reached on an obligatory submission of disputes to adjudication; instead an optional protocol was prepared allowing states to accept the jurisdiction of the International Court of Justice for the purpose of deciding any dispute relating to the interpretation or application of the four conventions adopted by the Conference. This protocol was accepted by less than forty states. In the United States, the Senate vote for it was only 49 to 30, thus falling short of the necessary two-thirds. 12 Whiteman, Digest of International Law 1333 (1971). Consequently, when disputes arose between the United States and Canada concerning pollution jurisdiction in the Arctic Ocean, the United States was not able to submit them to the Court.

The United States is further handicapped by the fact that its earlier acceptance of the jurisdiction of the International Court of Justice under the optional clause in Article 36 of the Statute of the Court was limited by two broad reservations: the so-called Connally Amendment (an amendment presented by the Senator from Texas, Chairman of the Committee on Foreign Relations, to the Senate resolution consenting to U.S. acceptance of jurisdiction), which excluded from the Court's jurisdiction all "disputes with regard to matters which are essentially within the domestic jurisdiction of the United States of America as determined by the United States of America"; and a reservation excluding from the Court's jurisdiction all "disputes arising under a multilateral treaty, unless (1) all parties to the treaty affected by the decision are also parties to the case before the Court, or (2) the United States of America specially agrees to jurisdiction." Declaration of August 14, 1946, 61 Stat. 1218 (1946). Under both clauses, the acceptance of the jurisdiction of the Court is in fact left to the discretion of the United States and, as the declarations under the optional clause are based on reciprocity, any other state may invoke these reservations against the United States at that state's discretion. This happened actually in a case between the United States and Bulgaria, where Bulgaria invoked the domestic jurisdiction clause though the issue—shooting down an Israeli airplane, with U.S. passengers on board—was clearly an international law matter. See Gross, "Bulgaria Invokes the Connally Amendment," 56 A.J.I.L. 357 (1962).

Taking this experience into account, from the very beginning of the negotiations leading to the LOS Convention, several states (including the

United States) have insisted that effective means be provided for settling law of the sea disputes. It was recognized that in such a complex document there will be many ambiguous compromises and conflicting provisions, which will require clarification and reconciliation through future decision-making. After difficult negotiations an intricate system for the settlement of law of the sea disputes was devised, which was spelled out in more than 100 articles scattered throughout the Convention and several annexes.

The guiding principle is that the will of the parties must prevail and that the parties may by agreement select any dispute settlement method they wish. They can bypass the provisions of the Convention by agreeing in advance to use some other bilateral, regional or general dispute settlement system. LOS Convention, Article 282. Even after a dispute has arisen and has been submitted to a procedure provided for in the Convention, the parties can agree "at any time" to settle it by a different procedure. Id., Article 280. Flexibility does not stop at this stage. Unlike most other international instruments, the LOS Convention does not provide for a unitary system of dispute settlement. As different groups of states desired different procedures, it was agreed that a state can choose one of four main systems of dispute settlement: the International Court of Justice, a special International Tribunal for the Law of the Sea, an international arbitral tribunal or a special technical arbitral tribunal. Id., Article 287(1). If the parties to a dispute have not accepted the same procedure, they are obliged to submit it to arbitration (id., Article 287(5)), and Annex VII to the Convention provides a foolproof method for selecting an arbitral tribunal. This dispute settlement system applies without any exception to the vast majority of the provisions of the Convention, but in order to obtain general consensus on this part of the Convention, three categories of disputes had to be subjected to different procedures.

First, some coastal states were not willing to accept strict dispute settlement provisions with respect to all disputes relating to the exercise by a coastal state of its sovereign rights or jurisdiction in the exclusive economic zone. It became necessary to subdivide these disputes into three groups: (a) disputes relating to violations by either the coastal state or any other state of the provisions of the Convention in regard to freedoms and rights of navigation, overflight, the laying of submarine cables and pipelines, or other internationally lawful uses of the sea, as well as disputes relating to violations by the coastal state of international rules and standards for the protection of the marine environment, remain subject to the general system for the settlement of disputes (id., Article 297(1)); (b) certain disputes relating to fisheries will be completely excluded from the dispute settlement system due to the broad discretionary powers of the coastal state with respect to several aspects of coastal fisheries; some other fishery disputes which involve the possibility of arbitrary actions of the coastal state will be subject to compulsory conciliation (resort to an international commission which can present a report on the facts and the law, which is not binding on the parties to the dispute but with which the parties usually comply); the remaining disputes will continue to be subject to the general system of dispute settlement (id., Article 297(3)); and (c) disputes relating to scientific research which are also subdivided into three subcategories, paralleling those relating to fishing (id., Article 297(2)).

Second, while the disputes relating to the exclusive economic zone discussed above are automatically exempt from dispute settlement procedures, another group of disputes may be excluded from dispute settlement procedures by filing a special optional declaration. The most complicated provisions relate to disputes concerning boundary delimitation or involving historic bays: old disputes, i.e., those which arose before the entry into force of the Convention, are totally exempt from disputes settlement under the Convention; new disputes, i.e., those which may arise after the entry into force of the Convention, will be subject to compulsory conciliation similar to that used for fishery and scientific research disputes; mixed disputes, i.e., disputes involving the concurrent consideration of sea boundaries and of any unsettled dispute concerning sovereignty over a part of the mainland or over an island or group of islands, will be totally exempt from dispute settlement under the Convention; and sea boundary disputes, which have been finally settled by an arrangement between the parties or which are to be settled in accordance with an agreement between them, will also be totally exempt from dispute settlement under the Convention. Id., Article 298(1)(a). There is also the possibility of a total exemption of disputes relating to two parallel activities: military activities (including military activities by government vessels and aircraft engaged in noncommercial service) and law enforcement activities by coastal states (if these activities are connected with those disputes involving fishing or marine scientific research which are themselves exempt from dispute settlement under Article 297(2) and (3)). Id., Article 298(1)(b). Finally, in order to avoid discrepant decisions by different international authorities, disputes which are being dealt with by the Security Council of the United Nations may be exempted (by an optional declaration) from dispute settlement under the Convention, but they will become again subject to Convention

procedures if the Security Council should cease
to deal with the matter. Id., Article 297(1)(c).

Third, most disputes relating to sea-bed mining are to be submitted to a special Sea-Bed Disputes Chamber of the International Tribunal for
the Law of the Sea in order to provide a uniform
system of interpretation for the part of the Convention which establishes a seabed mining regime.
That Chamber will be composed of eleven members to be chosen by the 21-member Tribunal
from among its membership. Id., Annex VI, Article 35. While the general dispute settlement
system applies only to disputes between states,
the Sea-Bed Disputes Chamber has jurisdiction
also over disputes between states and the International Sea-Bed Authority and, in contractual
matters, even disputes between the Authority and
both state and private enterprises. Id., Article
187. Some technical disputes relating to contracts may be submitted, however, to binding
commercial arbitration. Id., Article 188(2).
Similarly, commercial arbitration may be re-
sorted to in disputes relating to transfer of
seabed mining technology or to financial terms
of mining contracts. Id., Annex III, Articles 5(4)
and 13(15).

As the United States has announced that it will
not ratify the LOS Convention, it will not be
able to resort to the dispute settlement procedures provided for in the Convention even

[*245*]

with respect to those parts of the Convention which it considers as reflecting customary international law. The United States could perhaps file a supplementary declaration (in addition to that filed in 1946, discussed supra), by which it would accept the jurisdiction of the Court with respect to those rules of customary international law which have been codified in the LOS Convention, with the exception of parts dealing with deep seabed mining. Such a declaration would confer jurisdiction on the Court with respect to any dispute concerning these law of the sea matters with respect to any state which has accepted the jurisdiction of the Court under the optional clause without crippling reservations, i.e., some forty states. See 36 I.C.J.Y.B. 59–93 (1982). In this way the United States might be able to make its contribution to the subjection of the law of the sea disputes to the rule of law, thus avoiding the danger of escalation of law of the sea disputes into threats to international peace and the security of the United States.

# INDEX

# INDEX

# INDEX
## References are to Pages

[*249*]

# INDEX

# INDEX

[*252*]

# INDEX

## DEEPWATER PORTS

See also Artificial Islands and Installations

United States legislation, 148–149

## DELIMITATION

See also Baselines

Boundary dispute resolution, 77–78

Continental shelf, 64–76

Equidistance-special circumstance rule, 60–62, 65–67, 69–70, 72–73, 75

Equitable principles, 65–67, 69–70, 72–73, 75

Exclusive economic zone, 64–76

Historic title, effect on, 58–59, 60, 62–63

Provisional agreements, 64

Settlement of boundary disputes, 77–78, 243

Territorial sea, 60–63

United States' practice, 75–77

## DELTA

Baseline, 40

## DEVELOPING STATES

Access to exclusive economic zone living resources, 126

Deep seabed,

Economic assistance to developing country producers, 184

Participation in council, 181

Technology transfer, 182

Marine pollution standards, 195–196

## DISCHARGE

See Marine Environment

## DISPUTE SETTLEMENT

See Settlement of Disputes

## DOCUMENTATION

See Certificate, Nationality of Ships

## DRUG TRADE

Boarding of ship, 21

Cooperative agreements, 19, 21

United States legislation, 26

# INDEX
**References are to Pages**

# INDEX

[*257*]

# INDEX

# INDEX